MASTER RACE

Master Race

The Lebensborn Experiment in Nazi Germany

Catrine Clay and Michael Leapman

CORONET BOOKS
Hodder and Stoughton

First published in Great Britain in 1995 by Hodder & Stoughton
First published in paperback in 1996 by Hodder & Stoughton
A division of Hodder Headline PLC
A Coronet paperback

10 9 8 7 6 5 4 3 2 1

ISBN 0 340 66561 0

Printed and bound in Great Britain by
Cox & Wyman Ltd, Reading, Berkshire

Hodder and Stoughton
A division of Hodder Headline PLC
338 Euston Road
London NW1 3BH

Contents

List of Illustrations

The SS flag flies outside a Lebensborn home as babies are wheeled on to the terrace. (*Bundesarchive, Koblenz*)
The ritualised SS naming ceremony. (*Bundesarchive, Koblenz*)
A postcard stresses the rural character of the homes. (*Bundesarchive, Koblenz*)
Children playing in the fresh air. (*Bundesarchive, Koblenz*)
A poster is put up in a Polish village announcing an SS search. (*Bundesarchive, Koblenz*)
An SS officer offers chocolate to a baby. (*Bundesarchive, Koblenz*)
A searching soldier peers through a window as mother and child prepare to be resettled. (*Bundesarchive, Koblenz*)
Alexander Michelowski in 1946. (*From a private collection*)
Michelowski today. (*Private collection*)
A registration document for one of thousands of lost or unknown children showing the child's racial assessment. (*Private collection*)
Children being numbered and photographed from three angles. (*Warsaw Commission for Hitlerite Crimes*)
Werner Thiermann at age three and today. (*Private collection*)

Heinrich Himmler. (*Bundesarchive, Koblenz*)
A child has his head measured. (*Warsaw Commission for Hitlerite Crimes*)
Suitable prospective 'parents' examine a line of children. (*Warsaw Commission for Hitlerite Crimes*)
An unused racial testing document. (*Private collection*)
Children line up for inspection at Lodz, Poland. (*Warsaw Commission for Hitlerite Crimes*)
Alodia Witaszek and her sister Darya before being removed from home. (*Private collection*)
Alodia and her natural mother. (*Private collection*)
Cousins Leon and Alojzy Twardecki. (*Private collection*)
Alojzy aged ten. (*Private collection*)

Leon today. (*Ray Forsythe*)
Malgorzata Ratajczak revisits the railway station where she watched her son being taken away. (*Ray Forsythe*)
Alojzy and Malgorzata today. (*Ray Forsythe*)
Mounted Nazi troops on the lookout for likely Polish children. (*Bundesarchive, Koblenz*)

Introduction

As we passed the fiftieth anniversary of the end of the Second World War, much was written about the Holocaust. In newspapers, in magazines and on television, we were moved and sickened once again by the now familiar pictures from the concentration camps. Rightly so, for it is important that we should never forget.

Much less, though, has been written about the other side of the coin, the attempt by Nazi Germany to establish the Nordic Aryans as the master race through a breeding programme designed to eliminate genetic imperfection. Linked by the warped logic of a crazed moment in history, these twin aspects of Nazi racial policy were carried out by the same group of people. The carefully selected members of Himmler's élite SS corps hounded the Jews, herded them into ghettos and exterminated them in concentration camps. The same SS men were ordered to father the 'perfect Aryans' who would populate the Thousand Year Reich, and to steal from the occupied countries children who looked as if they might further improve the breed.

Nazi Germany was above all a racial state, driven by an ideology that demanded the purification of German blood. As Hitler and Himmler saw it, there were two parallel routes to the supreme goal: the racially impure had to be exterminated while the racially pure were encouraged to multiply. The Final Solution would be achieved only when both the negative and positive objectives had been fulfilled.

These ideas, extreme and unhinged though they now seem to most of us, did not emerge from a void. The concept that the world is split between the enlightened and lesser breeds was at the heart of Britain's rule of its empire. The theory of eugenics, of improving humankind by

ix

eliminating 'bad' genetic traits and breeding only from sound stock, had been around since the middle of the nineteenth century and was enthusiastically taken up in many parts of the world, notably the United States. It happened that it was the Nazis who had the technical means, the right political conditions and the total fanaticism to put them into practical effect. If it had not been them it could well have been someone else, for eugenics, though set back by the Nazis' failed experiment, has never gone away and is today undergoing something of a revival, if in a carefully sanitized form.

Struck by the comparative lack of discussion of this less horrific – if no less sinister – side of the Nazis' racial policies, I made two BBC Television documentaries that highlighted it. The first, *A Child for Hitler*, told the story of a woman born in one of the Lebensborn homes set up by the SS to provide the Reich with a steady supply of babies of good German blood. The SS fathers had already ascertained their impeccable Aryan ancestry as a condition for joining the corps and the mothers, to qualify, had to prove the same. The film explored the trauma of a daughter of one such 'perfect' liaison when she discovered, in early middle age, that her father was executed for war crimes.

The second documentary, *The Stolen Child*, was about the activities of the SS Race Office in the occupied territories; in this case Poland. Himmler's men kidnapped as many as 200,000 blond and blue-eyed Polish children, tested their racial credentials by individually measuring sixty-two parts of their bodies and, if they passed the tests, sent them away for 'Germanisation'. Many live in Germany to this day, unaware that they are Polish by birth.

In researching the films I became frustrated, recognising that in forty or fifty minutes of television there was no time to investigate every aspect of the ideology that gave rise to these extraordinary stories; neither its derivation nor the full consequences of its implementation. A chance meeting with the publisher Richard Cohen convinced me that the subject merited a book.

The great majority of books about this side of Nazi racial policy have been academic works, which have been of immense value to me and my co-author Michael Leapman in our researches on the subject. Our own book, however, is different. After explaining the essential background, we focus on individual cases, talking to the victims of the Nazis' racial obsession, men and women who were born out of these genetically correct couplings, or who were stolen from their homes as children. Where possible we have also spoken to their mothers, although many are now dead. Their stories are all moving personal tragedies that illustrate the terrible consequences of zealotry, of the pursuit of an obsession to what seems its logical conclusion. We conclude with a look at genetics today, examining whether the discredited racial ideas of the Nazis may insidiously be coming back into vogue.

Richard Cohen, whose idea it was, is the first person I want to thank. Roger Kingerlee, fresh from Oxford where he had clearly been every tutor's idea of the perfect student, became the perfect researcher. And Michael Leapman, seasoned journalist and writer, joined the team to show me the difference between writing a television commentary and writing between hard covers. Our main thanks, however, are owed to the many people who were prepared to tell us their scarcely credible stories. Alojzy and Leon Twardecki, the two cousins stolen from Poland on the same day, have been more than generous with their help and hospitality. Alojzy's mother, Malgorzata Ratajczek, now eighty-two, still lives in the same small town as when her son was taken. 'They stole my child,' she told us. 'He was four. My only child. I can't describe to you how it feels.'

Our thanks also to Alodia Witaszek-Napierara, Jan Tloczynski, Alexander Michelowski, and Dr Roman Hrabar, a member of the Polish mission who went in search of the stolen children at the end of the war. At eighty-four, he is still writing and lecturing on the subject, and was both a help and an inspiration. In Germany most people, understandably, preferred to remain anonymous but we received enthusiastic help from Freiherr Otto von Feury, who ran the Lebensborn home at Steinhöring on behalf of the Allies after the German surrender. In Norway, Werner Thiermann and his wife Mary were enormously hospitable and gave us access to his extensive archive on the Norwegian children of German soldiers. In London, Steve Jones helped steer me through the minefield of modern thinking on genetics. Finally, our thanks to Roland Philipps at Hodder and Stoughton for his helpful editorial suggestions.

Catrine Clay
London
Summer 1995

1

The House behind the Gates

For us the end of the war will mean an open road to the east, the creation of the Germanic Reich in one way or another . . . the fetching home of 30 million people of our blood, so that during our lifetime we shall be a people of 120 million Germanic souls. That means that we shall be the sole decisive power in Europe. That means that we shall be able to tackle peacetime, during which we shall be able for the first 20 years to rebuild and extend our towns and villages, and push the borders of our German race 500 kilometres farther out to the east.

Heinrich Himmler, 14 October 1943

The ten-man patrol from C Company, of the United States Army's 86th Infantry Division, swung quickly but warily down Münchener Strasse, the main street of the little village of Steinhöring, on the afternoon of 3 May 1945. Half of them were looking for trouble on the left-hand side of the road, the other half covered the right. They were coming towards the end of the village, with open country just ahead, when the left-hand group, alert for snipers, came to a pair of decorative iron gates next to a curious round white tower with a conical cap. Going through the gates, they moved carefully up a concrete drive to a substantial building in Bavarian style, with a steeply pitched roof. Sten guns at the ready, they kicked open the front door.

On the floor of a large sunny room, quite comfortably furnished, they found about forty babies and toddlers, some wailing and some quite silent, some dressed and some almost naked, but all obviously hungry and bewildered. In rooms upstairs were more babies and children, amounting to perhaps three hundred in all, from new-born to the age of six. There were a few mothers and some who would soon be giving birth, as well as a corps of young nurses, many of handsome appearance. The women were sullen and resentful at the Americans' intrusion and would not answer questions addressed to them in German. The soldiers had no way of knowing it then, but they had stumbled across the vestiges of the Nazis' grandiose scheme to populate Europe with a master race of Nordic peoples, specially bred to keep lesser mortals in subservience until gradually eliminating them.

The 86th, nicknamed the Black Hawks, were surging south and east in a broad arc east of Munich, the birthplace of the Nazi movement. Now they were heading towards Wasserburg and the Austrian border. Their route took them across the low green foothills of the Alps, past fields of sleepy cattle and emerging corn and through forests peopled by shadowy colonies of refugees – some local, others Russians and Poles who had been brought to southern Germany as slave labour. It was a fine day but a cloud of dust was drifting overhead, raised by shelling a mile or two beyond.

There had been no shooting in the village itself, even though they were approaching that part of southern Bavaria, close to the mountainous border with Austria, where the Allied commanders feared that the rump of the German army might stage a last-ditch stand. But the death of their Führer, Adolf Hitler, had been announced just the previous day and, in what were to be the last two days of the war, most of the inhabitants were resigned to the collapse of the German imperial dream. Many had hung white flags of surrender from the wood-framed windows of their chalet-style houses, decorated with the colourful boxes of geraniums that characterise Bavaria. Retreating German soldiers gathered in compounds established by the Americans at the roadside, to volunteer themselves as prisoners.

Only a few diehards – mostly members of the Hitler Youth and the élite SS and Parachute regiments – were putting up token resistance. There had already been one or two ambushes. That was why infantrymen of C Company were advancing carefully down Steinhöring's main street, searching buildings and other likely hideouts for snipers. They had been told little about the village, but there were suggestions that it contained an important institution connected with the SS – Himmler's cruel and secretive force that spearheaded the Nazi revolution. In the tense atmosphere, the calm of the village seemed eerie and the men were certainly in no mood to absorb its landmarks – the pretty church with a bulbous spire bearing the date 1902; and outside it the neat cemetery, some of its headstones carved in the crudely heroic style the Nazis championed.

Down a lane opposite the church was a small railway station. The Americans would not then have appreciated that the track, disappearing in a straight line to the north-west, headed direct to Dachau – a name they already knew as the place where the SS carried out its task of exterminating enemies of the Nazis, and which before long they and a horrified world would learn to identify with the regime's insane racial obsession.

The victorious troops should have been feeling elated but they were not. Had they known of Hitler's death and the imminent surrender it would have raised their morale, but they were away from their divisional base and the news had not reached them. 'What we mainly felt was tired,' one of the men recalled half a century later. 'Tired and hungry.'

Their route had taken them across many of the rivers that flow through this landscape, and the retreating Germans had destroyed all the bridges. While the infantrymen could wade across the water or use small boats, the supporting trucks with their supplies could not get through. When, two days earlier, they had crossed the River Isar at Freising – today the site of Munich's international airport – their supplies had been left behind. That meant that the advance foot-soldiers had effectively to live off the land, foraging for chickens, geese, eggs and last year's stored potatoes. 'We found what we could but it was never enough,' the veteran soldier remembered.

The big building on the left of the road was surrounded by a wall that also enclosed a lake and a large, well-tended garden. Near the entrance, beyond the white tower, was a bold, outsized, grey stone statue of a mother breast-feeding her baby. She was blessed with the regular classical features and strong physique that the Nazis thought characteristic of the Aryan race, her hair demurely tied into a soft bun at the nape of her neck. Hers was an heroic and idealised image, a concrete expression of the Nazi ideology of racial superiority.

As for the building itself, it could easily, from external appearances, have been a hospital, a school or some other benign institution. Yet it was none of those things and it was not immediately apparent to the men exactly what purpose it served. Had they known, they would have been reluctant to believe it.

If any of them were inclined to speculate, their thoughts were interrupted by the gruesome sight that confronted them at the entrance. On top of a large cart brimming with trash was the body of a German trooper lying face up, his feet in long leather boots hanging over the edge. Probably not many of the Americans were observant enough to notice, unobtrusively moulded on to the ornate iron gates of the house, the same symbol that the dead soldier wore on his black uniform – the stylised letters SS. After assuring themselves that he was really dead, they went in and found the children.

Steinhöring had been the first of Heinrich Himmler's Lebensborn homes (the word means 'fount of life'), where his meticulously planned breeding programme had begun nearly ten years earlier and where now, in defeat, the last pathetic remnants of this crazy attempt at genetic manipulation were huddled. The significance of the symbol on the gate was twofold. Firstly, although primarily medical and welfare centres, the homes were run on a strict regime by the SS, of which Himmler was leader (Reichsführer). More significantly this élite, hand-picked corps was to have been the prime begetter of the new Aryan nation. Its members would pass their unblemished warrior blood on to succeeding generations of Germans, thanks to the eager compliance of healthy young women who, after an equally rigorous selection process, had been pronounced of pure enough breeding to 'make a child for Hitler'. Hitler was now dead. The babies bawling in the Bavarian countryside would eventually have to cope with the trauma of his heritage.

Conscious of the disturbance they were causing, the Americans checked that there were no armed men in the home and quickly moved on. Within two days they had crossed the River Salzach at Berghausen and were in Austria, to be followed into Steinhöring by a second wave of Americans with the task of administering the defeated village.

In their rapid advance across West Germany, the occupying army had evolved a routine for doing this. The first thing was to look around for a local figure to act as a link with the occupying forces. While it was clearly difficult to evaluate people's true political sympathies at a time when the old orthodoxy had, overnight, become the new heresy, they sought somebody who had not been overtly and actively involved with the Nazi regime. At Steinhöring, at the suggestion of the priest, they appointed a local landowner, Freiherr Otto von Feury, partly because he was a quarter Jewish. At his suggestion the Americans chose a new mayor – Johann Grander, who ran the local dairy.

The fate of the Hochland (Highland) mother and baby home was not a priority with the villagers, who in the last days of the war had other things to worry about. The population of Steinhöring had more than doubled from about 1,000 to 2,500 as people arrived in flight from the Russian army in the north-east. There were shortages of food and accommodation, with householders forced to have refugees billeted on them. According to the consistent testimony of villagers since the war (which must be evaluated in the light of their understandable sensitivity to suggestions that they supported or collaborated with the Nazis) they felt separate from the home. This had been the case ever since it opened in 1936, in what had been a residence for priests and then, briefly, a training school for the SA, the unruly brown-shirted stormtroopers who had played a crucial role in bringing the Nazis to power.

As soon as Himmler took it over as a Lebensborn home he began work on an ambitious extension. He was obsessed with the practical detail of creating a fine, dignified and healthy environment for the mothers and future citizens of the Thousand Year Reich, resonant with German history and tradition. The buildings were to be based on the farmhouse style of Bavaria, where he had grown up. They would have steeply pitched roofs, balconies and French windows opening out on to long terraces, overlooking the idyllic Bavarian landscape. The rooms would be light and airy, decorated with Germanic symbols and ornaments. Even the diet would be based on Himmler's own enthusiasm for the new theories of nutritious and healthy eating.

The people of Steinhöring had been actively discouraged from taking much interest in the Hochland home and its occupants. The feared SS ran it as a state within a state, where secrecy was paramount. The mothers and nurses were seldom seen in the village, and when they were there they showed no interest in striking up friendships with the locals. Not that, even if they had fraternised, the farmers and shopkeepers of Steinhöring would have found much in common with the home's occupants, many of them secretaries and other working girls from the cities, and members of the BDM, the strongly Nazi League of German Girls. One villager said: 'The staff would come out and go to the butcher and get the meat, they'd go to the baker to get the bread and the dairy to get the milk; then they'd go in again.'

Things were not as simple as that for von Feury on that May morning, when he suddenly found himself in charge of around 350 babies in a home whose SS administrators and most of the medical personnel had abandoned it some forty-eight hours earlier. The shops were all closed. The Germans had taken vital supplies with them as they fled towards the Alpine redoubt where some of them still believed that a last-ditch defence could be mounted. The building normally housed no more than 150 people, but by now it was seriously overcrowded because mothers and babies from other Lebensborn homes in the path of the Allied advance, some in the former occupied territories, had been evacuated to it.

Of Steinhöring's full complement of sixteen nurses, only eight had remained with their charges. Most were from the notorious 'Brown Sisters', the fanatical group of Nazi women, officially welfare work-ers, who were responsible for many of the kidnappings of children in occupied territories which had formed a second plank of Himmler's racial strategy. Most of the mothers had left, too, partly because it was Lebensborn policy that they should not stay with their children for more than a few weeks after the birth if they did not plan to keep them.

Von Feury had first of all to find milk and bread for the children. Normal supplies had been disrupted by the American advance, which made it impractical for farm vehicles to reach the shops: that was why they were closed. Von Feury had an old car. By persuading the Americans of the urgency of the situation, he obtained petrol and permission to drive from farm to farm collecting milk and anything else to assuage the childrens' hunger.

His next task was to find a doctor, for the American invasion had not interrupted normal biological processes and several women in the home were due to give birth imminently. Here again the Americans gave him a hand. He knew of a Dr Kleinle in Wasserburg, twenty kilometres to the east, who had some pediatric experience. The Americans had interned him for suspected Nazi sympathies but in the emergency they were prepared to release him. It took nearly a fortnight to arrange, and until Kleinle arrived on 15 May the resident midwife, who had stayed with the children and mothers, took care of their medical needs. Some of the Brown Sisters who stayed were defiant in their loyalty to the Reich: one local story is that some had to be dismissed for singing Nazi songs in their upstairs quarters.

The arrival of the Americans can be traced intriguingly through the birth registers from the home, now held at Steinhöring village hall. The Lebensborns had conducted their own birth registration procedures almost since their inception, for Himmler thought it unwise to let the records of the beginnings of his new Germanic race get into non-SS hands. Although the names of the children's fathers were not normally mentioned on the birth certificates, many of them wrote a few words acknowledging paternity and accepting responsibility for the child.

Since such a document was of little value with no name attached, it is assumed that the name of the father was recorded separately, in records that could later be used to confirm the child's racial purity. All those records were destroyed: von Feury and others recall massive bonfires of documents in the 48 hours before the SS left Steinhöring, filling the air with smoke and an acrid stench. There is also a persistent story that the Americans themselves threw a lot of Lebensborn records into the river when they took the organisation's Munich headquarters.

The registration process was normally completed on the day the children were born, but the arrival of the Americans interrupted the routine. One baby born on 1 May was registered on that day but there were no further registrations until 5 May, when five births were recorded. Details of the mothers' background had become even more sketchy than hitherto. Most now gave their address simply as Steinhöring, suggesting that they may have been taken there from one of the other homes.

During the four-day gap another, more significant change occurred in the wording of the entries. The child's birthplace was no longer recorded as the Hochland Home – one of the romantically rural names that Himmler bestowed on the Lebensborn units to reinforce his dream of the new race springing from the heart of the traditional German homeland. Instead it was simply called 'the children's hospital'. In those four missing days, Himmler's dream ended.

*   *   *

The trouble with Nazi dreams was that the people caught up in them were not figments of a theorist's imagination but all too real. Few of the Steinhöring babies now in American care had their mothers with them and none had their fathers. Although the mother's name was known, the entries in the register, even of children born earlier in the war, seldom contained a useful address: often one of a handful of known SS addresses in Munich was used.

Some of the mothers had planned to bring their children up themselves, especially those who were married, and a few did return to collect their babies. The majority, having produced their child for Hitler, had disappeared, happy to give the baby up for adoption by a family selected by the SS. Clearly a couple thought by the Nazis to be suitable adoptive parents would, almost by definition, be unsuitable by the criteria of the occupying Americans. As for tracing the fathers, that was well nigh impossible: if they were members of the SS, as many were, they would either be in hiding, under arrest or dead.

Von Feury remembers that local people were reluctant to adopt children from an institution that they viewed with deep misgivings. Placing the children was therefore a slow process. Von Feury did what he could but it was three months before a team from the International Red Cross – the organisation to which much of this emergency clear-up work fell at the end of the war – was installed at the home and began to tackle the Herculean task in earnest. Later the Catholic charity Caritas, the United Nations Relief and Rehabilitation Administration, the International Refugee Organisation and the International Tracing Service all made efforts either to find a child's real parents or to have it suitably adopted. It took more than a year before all the children were settled. There were some successful placings but rather more failures, with some of the unluckiest children sent repeatedly from family to family and, in the case of those of foreign origin, from country to country. Von Feury recalls that one or two were adopted by men of the occupying American army. Most, though, ended up in institutions.

The home still gets visits from people born there, trying, usually in vain, to retrieve some meaningful link with their past, some clue as to who they are and where they came from. Nowadays there is an average of three or four such visits a year, but there was a spurt when the Iron Curtain was lifted and the division between West and East Germany ended.

Most of the returnees left the village so young that today they have no memory of it, but if they could remember they would find some features as they were then. The iron gates are still there, with the unobtrusive SS marking and the stylised scrollwork designs, representing the Lebensborn symbol and old Germanic runes beloved by Himmler as part of his ancestral dreams. The glass and iron lamps on the gateposts, and next to them the Gothic white tower, are similarly inspired by that romantic vision. The original building has been pulled down but Himmler's extension remains and is now itself being extended. The patio where the babies were put out in their cots, to drink in the healthy country air, still looks out over the peaceful lake and garden.

Inside, the rounded-off corners in the corridor are typical of 1930s architecture. The chandeliers in the hall, plain iron circles holding nine lamps, are also original, even if any symbolism in their design is long forgotten. You can still see the room used for the elaborate naming ceremony, a characteristic piece of SS hocus-pocus where a ceremonial sword, bigger than the baby itself, was placed on its stomach to the strains of Haydn's *Variations on the German Anthem*.

The former Lebensborn children have, in half a century, found their own separate ways of coming to terms with the circumstances of their birth. Revisiting the home helps satisfy their curiosity about their origins but at the same time focuses their mind on the dreadful scheme in which they were unwilling participants.

'I can't connect with it,' one of them said. 'Even though I was born with it I can't connect with it. The ideology was one thing. I was another.'

The Lebensborn project addressed only one aspect of Himmler's racial Utopia. So great was his desire to foster Aryan blood that he would have blond, healthy children stolen from their parents in all parts of the nascent Nazi empire and brought to the homeland for 'Germanisation'. These were clearly less satisfactory than the children produced in the Lebensborn homes from guaranteed stock, but when you are aiming at a target of 120 million plus, you have to make the odd compromise, especially if you are simultaneously losing people as well. For the plan had another, still darker side. Creating a master race meant systematically eliminating those who might compromise the purity of its blood – the Jews, the gypsies, the Slavs and those with hereditary physical or mental imperfections.

When Himmler took over the SS as Reichsführer in 1929, he told his men that the SS was 'the blood carrier which can make history'. He went on:

> 'Should we succeed in establishing this Nordic race again in and around Germany and inducing them to become farmers, and from this seed bed produce a race of 200 million, then the world will belong to us . . . We are called, therefore, to create a basis on which the next generation can make history.'

The presence of the five Americans on that May morning in Steinhöring represented the final assurance that this chilling vision would never materialise.

2

The Racial Utopia

The Nordic man is the active man of deeds, with a constant temperament and a withdrawn, cool, realistic nature. In his inclinations he is experimental, adventurous, aggressive, full of deep feelings, good nature and a sense of justice. He is characterised by his love of truth, honour, freedom and purity. He has a tough, decisive will and an objective, clear and goal-oriented organisational mind.

Anthropologist Egon von Eicksedt, 1934

Adolf Hitler's 1926 testament *Mein Kampf* had many faults, but ambiguity was not one of them. His vision of Germany's future was based clearly on a racial philosophy derived from the works of popular science – chiefly anthropology and genetics – that had become fashionable during the second half of the nineteenth century. A group of European thinkers, who came to be known as Social Darwinists, latched on to the theory of evolution and natural selection that Darwin first aired in his seminal work of 1859, *The Origin of Species*; but they extended and corrupted it to justify the racial engineering that attracted Hitler and which, in the Lebensborn homes and the death camps that complemented them, he put into effect.

The Social Darwinists were especially impressed with Chapter Three of *The Origin of Species*, which Darwin called 'The Struggle for Existence'. Its argument was that the species that survived and prospered were those that defended themselves fiercely against competitors. One of the chief weapons in their struggle was a rapid increase in numbers through intensive breeding. In 1871, in *The Descent of Man*, Darwin elaborated his theory and introduced the notion – crucial to the Social Darwinists – that nineteenth-century advances in civilisation, especially in medicine, would interfere with natural selection, ensuring the survival of the unfit as well as the strong, unless deliberate breeding programmes were introduced to balance their effect.

His followers went further, convincing themselves that, as mankind had become the dominant species through strengthening the features that distinguish humans from lesser beings and handing them down to succeeding generations, so it would be possible to enhance the race by deliberately choosing to breed from men and women whose qualities you wanted to see preserved. The corollary was the suppression, by extermination or enslavement, of people whose undesirable characteristics would pollute the mix.

The issue of racial differences had been controversial even before *The Origin of Species*. In 1855 the French count Arthur de Gobineau, in his *Essay on the Inequality of the Human Races*, declared that inherited racial characteristics rather than environmental factors were the driving force of human history. The white 'Aryan' race, he maintained, was superior to all others, its strength and bravery enhanced by a striking physique. (The original Aryans were Hindus but the name came to be used for the whole Indo-European family of languages and later the northern European racial type. In its racial context the word eventually became almost interchangeable with the terms Nordic and Germanic.)

Gobineau also formulated the theory that became the basis for the Lebensborn movement: that peoples such as the Greeks and Romans came to dominate the world because of their racial purity. Only when that purity was diluted by interbreeding did they degenerate and lose their vitality. Interbreeding, wrote Gobineau, should be avoided at all costs. Hitler agreed. He wrote in *Mein Kampf*: 'History ... shows with terrifying clarity that in every mingling of Aryan blood with those of lower peoples, the result was the end of the cultured people.' So what more natural than to ensure the perpetual dominance of the cultured people by ensuring that they only mated with each other?

The sub-text of all these theories was anti-Semitism, a force in Europe since the Middle Ages, when Jews had settled in large cities and engaged in a variety of commercial and professional activities, especially finance and medicine. Fierce guardians of their social and religious traditions, and with a distinctive physical appearance, the Jews became an easy target for populist, rabble-rousing and ambitious political agitators. In 'proving' that the Aryan race was genetically superior, the Social Darwinists and their successors were consigning the Jews and other non-Aryans to a definable lower order of being. From there it was a comparatively short step to the Nazis' Nuremberg Laws of the 1930s, barring Jews from wide areas of German life and forbidding intermarriage; then another step, scarcely longer, to the concentration camps.

Darwin's book sparked a boom in racial anthropology. Researchers used instruments such as callipers and craniometers to measure heads, brains, noses and other parts of the anatomy. Skulls were weighed, bones examined, hair and eye colourings meticulously noted. The Swedish anthropologist Anders Retzius introduced a 'cephalic index' which attached significance to the combined measurement of the length and breadth of the skull. The possibility of detecting criminal tendencies through the shape of the head was solemnly discussed (a precursor of today's quest for 'the criminal gene'). The German Society for Anthropology set up a commission to determine the racial composition of the German states, and by 1885 an estimated 15 million children had been measured. One enthusiastic researcher was said to have made 5,000 measurements of a single skull.

Francis Galton, a cousin of Darwin, was among the first to propagate Social Darwinist views and, in 1883, to coin the word 'eugenics' to describe the science (for such he believed it to be) of using genetics to improve racial quality. The word literally means 'breeding well'. Believing that natural ability was hereditary, Galton advocated that people of achievement should be issued with certificates of racial health and encouraged to marry young and have large families. At the same time he was worried about the high fertility of the poor. He elaborated the theory that advances in medicine helped weaken racial stock by ensuring the survival of sick and fragile people who would have perished if nature had been allowed to take its course. One answer, he believed, would be to discourage or prevent people of low racial value from breeding; or they could be persuaded to emigrate to the colonies.

In 1904 Galton founded the National Eugenics Laboratory and soon afterwards the Eugenics Education Society, among whose objectives was the sterilisation of the insane and feeble. Parallel institutions sprang up in parts of the United States, where a Eugenics Records Office was set up to co-ordinate research, with the financial backing of the highly respectable Rockefeller and Carnegie foundations. It was not long before eugenics was used to justify racial selection of US immigrants.

Ideas about the master race were received especially warmly in Germany, where they were seen as a possible answer to the severe social problems caused by rapid industrialisation and population growth in the second half of the nineteenth century. Ernst Haeckel, Professor of Zoology and later of Social Anthropology at the University of Jena, was an early adherent of Social Darwinism. In 1869 he was supporting Gobineau's argument that the people of central Europe were superior to others and had created all that was worthwhile in culture. (He had narrowed Gobineau's classification of the master race as Aryans to 'West Aryans', or the Germanic people.) Haeckel believed that a race was comparable to a biological organism, in that its overall well-being was dependent on the health of its constituent parts. By 1904 he was attacking organised religion and, like Galton, advocating the systematic elimination of the weak and sick. In his book *Die Lebenswunder*, Haeckel wrote:

> What profit does humanity derive from the thousands of cripples who are born each year, from the deaf and dumb, from cretins, from those with incurable hereditary defects, etc., who are kept alive artificially and then raised to adulthood? What an immense aggregate of suffering and pain those depressing figures represent for the unfortunate sick people themselves, what a fathomless sum of worry and grief for their families, what a loss in terms of private resources and costs to the state for the healthy!

The device of pleading social concern as a justification for implementing measures of racial hygiene was a tempting one. Later, Himmler and the other advocates of the Lebensborn homes would claim to be motivated to help under-privileged mothers. Sterilisation and euthanasia, too, have often been represented as measures to help the poor and ease pain. In Nazi propaganda films, euthanasia was presented as 'mercy killing'.

Haeckel was also one of the first to link racial purity with a return to a natural open-air lifestyle – a reaction against the increasing squalor of the diseased and crowded cities. He would take his students on long walks in the Thuringian hills, where they would discuss Darwin's theories and the freedom of the spirit.

His work was absorbed and developed by his successor in the chair of Social Anthropology at Jena, Alfred Ploetz, who invented the notion of 'racial hygiene' (*Rassenhygiene*). In 1879, when only nineteen, Ploetz and a group of friends, including the playwright Gerhard Hauptmann, established the League to Invigorate the Race. It was a symptom of the growing spirit of nationalism – and its corollary anti-Semitism – that swept Germany towards the end of the nineteenth century. The League advocated some curious practices, including wearing only clothes made from fibres derived from a mammal: because this is the species to which man belongs, it was believed that the practice would improve both mental and physical health. The League also forbade the use of alcohol, not out of concern for the health and well-being of users but because it was seen as damaging to the racial stock.

In his later writings on race, Ploetz developed the theory that, because improvements in social welfare increased the survival rate of the poorest and least fit members of society, a positive breeding programme was required to ensure that the best and most healthy racial characteristics were not buried. In 1905 he was one of the founders of the Racial Hygiene Society, Germany's first society openly to espouse eugenics. Its members were drawn from the professional classes and had to undergo an anthropological examination to determine whether they were truly Aryan. Once they had passed it, they were encouraged to breed profusely, with the object of strengthening the stock of what in horses would be called thoroughbreds, to prevent alien cells from entering the pure Aryan blood and contaminating it. Several other small groups with similar aims were formed in Germany in the first decade of the century.

In 1912 a more influential organisation, the Thule Society, was created, with important unofficial backing from the military. Taking its name from Ultima Thule, reputed to be the birthplace of the German race, it was a highly selective society which, like the Racial Hygiene Society, also imposed strict criteria for membership, including proof of pure Aryan blood for at least three generations – a requirement later incorporated into Nazi breeding programmes. Its blunt slogan was: 'Remember you are German! Keep your blood pure!'

The Society, apart from organising lectures and meetings, undertook anti-communist political activity and sponsored the German

Workers Party, which Hitler joined before it changed its name to the German National Socialist Workers Party. The new initials, NSDAP, soon led to its being known as the Nazi party – whose swastika symbol derived from the Thule Society, as did its main political aim of uniting Europe under German leadership.

The year 1912 was a landmark in the eugenics movement for another reason: the first International Congress of Eugenics was held at London University in July, with Ploetz as one of its main participants. It brought together three hundred enthusiasts of the emerging movement from Europe and the United States, including such influential names as Charles Davenport, Director of the Eugenics Record Office at Cold Spring Harbor, Long Island. The prestige of eugenics was illustrated by the eminence of the non-specialists who attended: the inventor of the telephone, Alexander Graham Bell; the presidents of Harvard and Stanford Universities; and Winston Churchill, First Lord of the Admiralty.

Among subjects discussed at the meeting were measures to restrict the reproduction of low-grade people and encourage the multiplication of better-quality stock. The United States was much admired for leading the world in the matter of sterilisation of the mentally handicapped. Indiana had enacted a law allowing this in 1907, and by the time of the conference similar laws existed in California, Connecticut, Nevada, Iowa, New Jersey and New York. The following year Kansas, Michigan, North Dakota and Oregon joined the bandwagon.

However, not all German eugenicists thought that sterilisation on its own was an adequate measure. The most influential of those who wanted a more interventionist approach was Fritz Lenz, who became Germany's first Professor of Racial Hygiene at the University of Munich in 1923. (It remained the only university to embrace this discipline until the Nazis achieved power in 1933. By 1936 nine other German universities had opened similar departments and all the others taught racial hygiene in their medical faculties. By this time the universities had themselves set a practical example of racial hygiene by purging their Jewish professors.)

Lenz believed that sterilisation would have a minimal effect on increasing the quality of the racial stock in Germany or anywhere else so long as the more 'capable' sections of society refused to multiply in adequate numbers. It was much more important, he maintained, to encourage breeding among those whose qualities you valued, rather than to take the purely negative step of slowing the birthrate of undesirables.

With the geneticist Erwin Baur and the anthropologist Eugen Fischer, Lenz was co-author of the seminal German textbook on racial matters: *An Outline of Human Genetics and Racial Hygiene*, published in 1921. In the second volume, which Lenz wrote on his own, he went into detail about the distinctions he saw between the sexes as well as the races:

> Men are specially selected for the control of nature, for success in war and the chase in the winning of women; whereas women are specially selected as breeders and rearers of children and as persons who are successful in attracting the male ... Hence arise the essential differences between the sexes.

Comparing the races, Lenz maintained that black people were intellectually inferior and lacked foresight. Jews were 'a mental race' interested in sex and medicine but, though precocious and witty, not truly creative – more adept at interpreting knowledge than at original thinking: 'Jews cannot transform themselves into Germans by writing books on Goethe,' he declared. As for the Nordic races, he praised them for their artistic leanings, their capacity for work, their realism and objectivity and their willingness to obey orders. Reviewing *An Outline of Human Genetics and Racial Hygiene* in the *New Statesman and Nation* in 1931, the English writer L. A. G. Strong called it 'a magnificent textbook ... a masterpiece of objective research and cautious hypothesis'. Hitler is believed to have read it in the Landberg prison after the attempted beer-hall putsch of 1923.

By the mid-1920s there was a raft of books devoted to the superiority of the Nordic race. H. F. K. Günther, in his *Ethnology of the German Nation*, wrote:

> The man of Nordic race is not only the most gifted but also the most beautiful. There stands the slim figure of the man, raised up to a triumphant blend of bone and muscle on a magnificent scale – the broad, powerful shoulders, the wide chest and narrow hips. The woman has slim, rounded shoulders and broad yet slender curved hips ... The man's face is hard and chiselled,

the woman's tender, with rose-pink skin and bright triumphant eyes – a sovereign race.

The theories on which Hitler's credo was based seem so extreme and lunatic today that it is difficult to imagine that they were ever taken seriously. Yet the climate of thought in the first years of the twentieth century was very different. Philosophers and social theorists in all Western countries were looking for new ways of organising a society they believed was collapsing into chaos as a consequence of rapid industrialisation and the unequal distribution of global wealth. While the eugenicists and racial hygienists were far from constituting a majority, there was an influential and respectable body of opinion prepared to give their views a rational hearing.

In Britain, these included the popular writer H. G. Wells. His 1901 work *Anticipations* contained thoughts that could have sat equally well in *Mein Kampf*. Describing his ideal society, Wells wrote:

The ethical system which will dominate the world state will be shaped primarily to favour the procreation of what is fine and efficient and beautiful in humanity – beautiful and strong bodies, clear and powerful minds and a growing body of knowledge – and to check the procreation of base and servile types ... The method that must in some cases still be called in to the help of man is death ... For a multitude of contemptible and silly creatures, fear-driven and helpless and useless, unhappy or hatefully happy in the midst of squalid dishonour, feeble, ugly, inefficient, born of unrestrained lusts and increasing and multiplying through sheer incontinence and stupidity, the men of the New Republic will have little pity and less benevolence.

His scorn was not restricted to the congenitally inadequate, but was spiced by a strong element of racism. He wrote of removing the racial identity of Jews, with their 'incurable tendency to social parasitism'. He went on:

For the rest – those swarms of black and brown and yellow people who do not come into the needs of efficiency? Well, the world is not a charitable institution and I take it they will have to go.

It is an indication of the climate of opinion at the time that Wells's book was not universally denounced when it appeared – though nor, to be fair, was it rapturously acclaimed. Other notable writers had also flirted with such views, Virginia Woolf, T. S. Eliot and even George Bernard Shaw among them. Marie Stopes, the birth control campaigner, was President of the Society for Birth Control and the Progress of Race, and attended the International Congress for Population Science in Berlin in 1935. The congress gave an important fillip to Nazi racial policies. A leading American eugenicist, Clarence Campbell, said in his address before it:

> The leader of the German nation, Adolf Hitler, ably supported by the Minister of the Interior, Dr Frick, and guided by the nation's anthropologists, its eugenicists and its social philosophers, has been able to construct a comprehensive race policy of population development and improvement that promises to be epochal in racial history. It sets the pattern which other nations and other racial groups must follow.

Many academics sought to give credence to eugenic theories – the notorious nude 'posture photographs', taken of American undergraduates at Ivy League colleges from the 1930s to as late as the 1960s and exposed in 1995, had their roots in a project that sought to prove that you could judge intellect and temperament from physical characteristics. Only when the Nazis began in earnest to put these and related racial theories into effect were their appalling implications fully appreciated.

The writer who made the most impact on Hitler was Houston Stewart Chamberlain, an Englishman living on the Continent, married to the daughter of the composer Richard Wagner – another devotee of the philosophy of Aryan supremacy. Chamberlain believed that mankind was organised into a strict hierarchy of racial types that had to breed only from within their own race if they were to avoid losing their identity through mongrelisation. In *The Foundations of the Twentieth Century*, published in Munich in 1899 (which Wells is also known to have read), Chamberlain argued that the Teutonic or Aryan race was the architect of European civilisation. He shared with Wagner and like-minded thinkers the view that Christ was not a Jew but the illegitimate son of a Roman legionary. Every major achievement of Western culture – the Italian Renaissance for example – he ascribed almost by definition to the Teutonic race.

The golden age of Greece, wrote Chamberlain, was the 'lost ideal, which we must strive to recover', but, like Rome, it had declined because of racial degeneration, just as today the Germanic people's future was threatened by mixing Aryan blood with that of other races. He believed the Jews were the chief offenders, trying deliberately and methodically to undermine the 'superior' Aryans through intermarriage, so as 'to infect Indo-Europeans with Jewish blood'. Although impressed by the strict Jewish social codes, he defined the aim of the Jew as being to 'put his foot upon the neck of all the nations of the world and be lord and possessor of the whole earth'.

Like Lenz, Chamberlain found special qualities in the Aryan, many of them the precise antithesis of those displayed by the Jew. Aryans were mystical, idealistic, loyal, cultured and free from corruption. In the book's last chapter, he attributed all the great achievements from the thirteenth to the nineteenth centuries to the Teutonic race, and advocated the improvement and purifying of the race through selective breeding and the systematic exclusion of foreign blood from the mix.

Hitler was so taken with these views that he idolised Chamberlain and insisted on being by his bedside at his death in 1927. In *Mein Kampf* he translated Chamberlain's philosophy into a two-pronged programme for action. Its negative aspect, the extermination of the Jews, was by far the more terrible and has rightly been examined and denounced exhaustively. The second strand, the enhancement and enlargement of the German race, was intended as the positive element and has been commented on less. Echoing Chamberlain, Haeckel, Gobineau and Lenz, Hitler wrote:

> The products of human culture, the achievements in art, science and technology with which we are confronted today, are almost exclusively the creative product of the Aryan. That fact enables us to draw the conclusion that he alone was the founder of higher humanity and was thus the very essence of what we mean by the term 'man'.

In Hitler's view the prime importance of history was as a record of the rise, conflict and fall of racial groupings; he feared that the

Jewish race would rise remoreslessly unless positive action was taken to strengthen the Aryans. These ideas played a central part in his territorial ambitions which led to the Second World War. The new Aryans would, if bred in the numbers he envisaged, require an extension of boundaries (*Lebensraum*) to create a greater German state. Thus he wrote in *Mein Kampf* of his aim 'to secure for the German people the land and the soil to which they are entitled on this earth at the expense of Russia and the vassal border states'. To ensure the purity of the race and its dominance over Europe – which would mean reversing the provisions of the Versailles Treaty after the First World War – was the central objective of his political and military strategy and remained so until, recognising finally that it could not be achieved, he committed suicide as the Allies entered Germany in 1945.

'What we must fight for', he wrote in *Mein Kampf*, 'is to safeguard the existence and reproduction of our race and our people, the sustenance of our children and the purity of our blood, the freedom and independence of the Fatherland, so that our people may mature for the fulfilment of the mission allotted it by the Creator.' He cited the laws of nature to support the argument for racial hygiene:

> Animals only mate with those of their own species. The titmouse seeks the titmouse, the finch the finch, the stork the stork, the field mouse the field mouse, the dormouse the dormouse, the wolf the she-wolf, etc.

Crossing a strong human being with a weak one would, he argued, produce a child of a level midway between that of the parents.

> The offspring will probably stand higher than the racially lower parent but not as high as the higher one ... Such mating is contrary to the will of Nature for a higher breeding of all life ... Inferior species are always numerically larger than superior species. Nature ensures that many of the inferior species go to the wall through harsh living conditions. The struggle ensures that only the healthiest males win the females, so the superior species increases. If Nature does not desire the mating of weaker with stronger individuals, even less does she desire the blending

of a higher with a lower race since, if she did, her work of higher breeding over perhaps hundreds of thousands of years would be ruined with one blow.

To breed between races, Hitler maintained, was therefore to rebel against the laws of nature and the principles to which man owed his very existence. To argue against this view – what he called the 'modern pacifist' objection – was to prescribe eventual doom for mankind, an argument he characterised as 'truly Jewish in its effrontery'. He declared:

Everything we admire on this earth today – science and art, technology and inventions – is only the creative product of a few peoples and originally perhaps one race. On them depends the existence of this whole culture. If they perish, the beauty of this earth will sink into the grave with them . . . All great cultures of the past perished only because the originally creative race died out from blood poisoning . . .
Blood mixture and the resultant drop in the racial level is the sole cause of the dying out of old cultures; for men do not perish as a result of lost wars but by the loss of that force of resistance which is contained only in pure blood. All who are not of good race in this world are chaff. And all occurrences in world history are only the expression of the races' instinct for self-preservation . . . Those who want to live, let them fight.

As he explored further these received notions of history, Hitler found in them the pretext for the master race exploiting the benighted:

For the formation of higher cultures the existence of lower human types was one of the most essential preconditions, since they alone were able to compensate for the lack of technical aids without which a higher culture is inconceivable. It is certain that the first culture of humanity was based less on the tamed animal than on the use of lower human beings . . . Hence it is no accident that the first cultures arose in places where the Aryan, in his encounters with lower peoples, subjugated them and bent them to his will.

He had no doubt who were the principal villains and, in a famously vivid paragraph, he described exactly how the Jews planned to achieve their ends:

> With satanic joy on his face, the black-haired Jewish youth lurks in wait for the unsuspecting girl whom he defiles with his blood, thus stealing her from her people. With every means he tries to destroy the racial foundations of the people he has set out to subjugate.

This is an extreme statement of a prejudice by any standards, but it is important to remember that in the climate of the early 20th century only the image would have been regarded as extreme. Casual anti-Semitic remarks were a routine part of discourse in social and business circles in Britain and elsewhere in Europe and crop up in the literature of the time – notably in Rudyard Kipling's bitterly anti-Semitic poem, *Gehazi*.

Even after the fanatical pursuit of this racial vendetta had led Germany and the world to an unimaginable disaster, Hitler never moderated his view. His death-bed testimony, dictated just before he committed suicide on 30 April 1945, ended: 'Above all, I enjoin the leadership of the nation to adhere to scrupulous observance of the race laws and merciless resistance to the world-poisoner of all peoples, international Jewry.' A hatred that can justify the killing of millions, and in the end is worth the sacrifice of his own life, is a powerful hatred indeed.

Hitler continued to be an avid reader of books on eugenics during and after the Nazis' climb to power. At least two American writers, Madison Grant and Leon Whitney, received letters from him congratulating them on their works, respectively *The Passing of the Great Race* and *The Case for Sterilization*. They reinforced the principles he expressed in *Mein Kampf*, principles from which his domestic and foreign policies flowed naturally. These policies, in turn, received support from eugenicists, especially in the United States, even after the start of the Second World War and the pogroms against the Jews. In the winter of 1939–40 the American eugenicist T.U.H. Ellinger paid a visit to leading racial research institutions in Germany. In an article in the *Journal of Heredity* he wrote coolly of the measures against the Jews as 'a large-scale breeding project, with the purpose of eliminating from the nation the hereditary aspects of the Semitic race'. He noted the 'amazing amount of unbiased information' about the Jews and their characteristics amassed by the Kaiser Wilhelm Institute.

As for the British, Hitler did not initially regard them as enemies: he admired Britain's basic Anglo-Saxon racial composition as opposed to that of France, with its obvious Mediterranean element. He approved, too, of the British Empire, especially those parts of it – for example, India and South Africa – where attempts were already being made to classify people on the basis of their race. It is worth recalling that the British also disapproved of intermarriage and its resultant 'half-castes' who compromised the purity of the race. Anglo-Indians were not allowed into British clubs – unless they were light-skinned enough to 'pass for white' – and their job prospects were limited. Men were restricted mainly to the army or police, where they did the colonial power's dirty work of keeping the natives under control. The young women, dubbed 'B-class girls', were similarly barred from professional or administrative positions, although they could become nurses or secretaries.

Because of this perceived identity of purpose, Hitler initially sought an alliance with Britain to conquer the Soviet Union and the rest of Europe. As the number of pure-blooded Germans increased through a domestic breeding programme, and through the introduction of fresh stock from elsewhere, their domain would extend to other parts of the world, where native peoples would be enslaved – the British Empire model again. In the long term the superior racial characteristics of the Germans would ensure world domination. For as long as biological stability was maintained, interracial conflicts would cease and that stage of world history would end.

New political parties fail much more often than they succeed. When they do achieve power it is because they have hit upon a theme that seems to address what people perceive as their most vital grievances and concerns. It was clear that Hitler had done that when *Mein Kampf*, after a slow start, became a huge bestseller in the 1930s; for Germany, at the beginning of the twentieth century, was racked both with grievances and concerns.

It was hard to believe that only a generation earlier Bismarck had delivered self-respect and a measure of unity, for the first time in centuries, to the former loose federation of weak and backward principalities. He had created an army, led by the élite Prussian officer corps, that briefly brought stability and prosperity to the nation through victories over Austria and France. At the same time the economy had been transformed and Germany rivalled Britain as the industrial powerhouse of Europe.

When Kaiser Wilhelm II dismissed Bismarck in 1890, that stability began to weaken. Industrialisation had led to overcrowding in the cities, with an increase in crime and disease – circumstances in which extreme socialist and communist movements have traditionally flourished. Seeking scapegoats for their misfortunes, many Germans pointed the finger at the communists on the one hand, and on the other at the Jewish community of shopkeepers, financiers, doctors and intellectuals.

Kaiser Wilhelm sought to mask the problems by emulating Bismarck's military successes, but instead he led Germany to defeat in the debilitating First World War, sacrificing millions of its young men. Wilhelm was forced to abdicate and the Weimar Republic was established, but the humiliating terms of the Versailles Treaty, involving huge reparations and the forfeiture of Alsace-Lorraine, provoked unrest in Germany. This reached ever more dangerous levels as massive inflation wiped out the savings of the middle class, whose peace of mind was already-disturbed by the success of the Bolshevik Revolution in Russia and the encouragement this had given to German communists.

These were ideal conditions for a political party preaching anti-Semitism and anti-communism. Adolf Hitler, the son of an Austrian customs official, had become interested in politics as an unemployed twenty-year-old in 1909, allying himself with parties that espoused both those creeds in the extreme. When the war began he volunteered for the army and in 1918 won the Iron Cross (first class) for bravery. In October that year, a month before the armistice, he was temporarily blinded in a British gas attack.

After a brief flirtation with communist revolutionaries, Hitler joined the army's 'propaganda commando', created to counter communist and socialist influence in the ranks. To train for this assignment he was sent on a course in which he learned the skills of oratory and agitation that were later to stand the Nazis in good stead. He found he had a natural flair for them. As part of his unorthodox military duties, he attended his first meeting of the infant Nazi Party in September 1919. Less than a year later, when he left the army, he joined the party as its 555th member. But he still kept close links with his old service colleagues, especially with Ernst Röhm, a captain whose job was to monitor paramilitary organisations that might be brought under the army's umbrella in the event of a new European conflict. In fact, Röhm was secretly and illicitly supporting some of these movements with army funds.

Within months Hitler had become the head of the party's propaganda machine and was recognised as its most compelling public speaker. An observer described him as 'a born orator, who with his fanaticism and popular manner compels the listener to attention and agreement'. According to records kept by the German army, in his first year of party membership he gave over half the speeches and lectures at its meetings. His themes included: 'Germany in her darkest hour', 'The Jewish question' and 'Might and right'.

Hitler quickly moved into a position of power. By 1921 he was President of the party and displayed – for the first but not the last time – his skill in ruthlessly sweeping aside any rivals for leadership. For a while he moved to Berlin to develop support in northern Germany in addition to that which he enjoyed in his Bavarian stronghold. He was especially interested in the party's paramilitary arm, the *Sturmabteilung*, or SA, which began to engineer street demonstrations and confrontations with communist supporters. Before long Hermann Göring, a former fighter pilot, had become the SA leader.

The Nazis were only one of a number of extreme right-wing parties with diverse aims: some wanted the restoration of the German monarchy, others sought independence for the principality of Bavaria. Initially membership of these parties was low but they all received a fillip in 1923, when the French and Belgian occupation of the Ruhr triggered strikes and sabotage which in turn led to the massive inflation. Membership of the Nazi Party increased from thousands to tens of thousands. When Heinrich Himmler joined in August 1923, he was given the number 42,404.

Himmler was born on 7 October 1900. His father Gebhard was a Munich schoolmaster who, although not active in politics, sympathised with Bavarian nationalism as a romantic concept. For a while Gebhard was tutor to the Bavarian Prince Heinrich: as well as being the young Himmler's namesake, the Prince also became his godfather.

From his father, Heinrich Himmler inherited a passion for detail and for meticulous annotation of his thoughts and activities. Gebhard collected stamps and coins and kept a careful record of his acquisitions. Heinrich was a keen collector, too, and from the age of ten kept a daily diary and later a reading list that historians have pored over for clues to his later infamy. In fifteen years he listed 270 books, including many on anthropology, heredity, genetics and racial hygiene. In his progress through the ranks of the Nazi Party, Himmler was noted for taking a close personal interest in details that might have been thought too small for the attention of someone in his powerful position.

As a child he was sickly, with a recurring lung infection, and he was not long into adolescence before he began suffering from the stomach cramps that plagued him all his life. Physically he was unimpressive – slight, ungainly and short-sighted, very far from the Aryan ideal. (It is an irony that scarcely any of the Nazi leaders would have passed their own racial tests: Hitler was no blond beauty, Goebbels was deformed, Göring overweight, Bormann bandy-legged, and Hess probably mad.)

Heinrich did well at school but from an early age decided that he did not want to follow his father's profession as a teacher. He was fourteen at the start of the First World War and the ensuing patriotic fervour inspired him to seek a military career. In 1917, after a few hurtful rebuffs, he was accepted as a cadet in the 11th Bavarian Infantry; but the German war effort collapsed before he finished his training and within a year he was a civilian again.

He became an agricultural student, although his experience on the practical side of the course was discouraging: a month after arriving at the farm where he was to train, he was taken to hospital with a paratyphus infection. This was when he began his reading list, complete with his thoughts on the books that figured on it. Among his early reading was Friedrich Wichtl's *World Freemasonry, World Revolution, World Republic*, which argued that the Jews, freemasons and Roman Catholics had combined in a plot to take over the world. It was, Himmler noted, 'a book which explains everything and tells us against whom we first have to fight'. He was less pleased with Dr Albert Daiber's *Eleven Years a Freemason*, commenting: 'A book without any particular revelations about freemasonry, presenting it only as terribly harmless.' He followed these with two anti-Semitic novels called *The Sins against the Blood* and *Ultimo*, commenting that the latter, which featured an unscrupulous Jewish banker, 'characterised the Jews very well'.

Although anti-Semitism was clearly a strong factor in his world view from the beginning, one or two comments on the reading list suggest that he was prepared to look at the Jewish question with at least the semblance of objectivity. After reading Arthur Dinter's *The Sins against the Blood* in 1920 he decided it was 'a tendentious work with anti-semitic intentions' and described the author as being 'in a blind fury in his hate for the Jews'. His objection was probably that the book amounted to a rant rather than a properly argued analysis.

Two years later he read Houston Stewart Chamberlain's *Race and Nation*, which appears to have been decisive in setting his views in concrete. He saw it as 'a convincing truth', noting: 'It is objective and not hate-filled anti-semitism. Thus it is all the more effective . . . this atrocious Jewry.'

In 1923 he devoured Theodor Fritsch's *Handbook of the Jewish Question* and enthused: 'It is a handbook in which one can find everything relevant. Even an initiate shudders when he reads it with understanding. If only some of the eternally unteachable could have it in front of them.' A year later he read Ernest Renan's *The Life of Jesus* and concluded: 'Christianity was and is the most outstanding protest of the Aryans against Jewry, of good against evil.'

At the same time he was reading books that lauded the Nordic race, such as Hans Günther's *The Knight, Death and the Devil*, which, he found, 'expresses in wise, considered language what I have felt and thought since I could first think'. On the other hand Oscar Wilde's *The Priest and the Acolyte*, with its references to homosexuality, put him in 'a frightful mood'.

Himmler completed his agricultural course in the summer of 1922 and went to work for a company near Munich making fertilisers for farms. In the months that followed, he involved himself ever more deeply in a number of right-wing political groups and became a dedicated admirer of Ernst Röhm, who probably influenced his decision to join the Nazis. A month after he had done so, Himmler quit his job at the fertiliser factory. His course to political power was set.

Two months later, on the night of 8 November 1923, he took part in the notorious beer-hall putsch, led by Hitler and Röhm, who had left the army in September. The Nazis and their supporters marched on the Munich hall, where the Bavarian Government were holding a political rally, and Hitler announced the formation of an alternative administration. Photographs show Himmler alongside Röhm and carrying the imperial German ensign in a demonstration of support for the attempted putsch; but it was defeated and the Nazi Party banned. Hitler spent eight months in prison.

When he was released the ban on the party was lifted, following an election in Bavaria in which nationalist groups had done badly. One Nazi who did win a seat in the *Landtag* was Gregor Strasser, who ran the SA in Lower Bavaria. Himmler had been given a job as Strasser's secretary: an enthusiastic motor-cyclist, one of his tasks was to travel to the SA's secret arms caches in the area and check their security and preparedness for action. According to an account by his brother Otto, Strasser thought Himmler the 'perfect arms NCO' but added: 'He looks like a half-starved shrew.'

Looks notwithstanding, Himmler rose quickly in the Nazi hierarchy. Later in 1924 he was appointed Strasser's deputy as leader of the party in southern Bavaria. In 1926 he was transferred to party headquarters in Munich as deputy head of propaganda, bringing him for the first time into day-to-day contact with Hitler. In September the following year he was made deputy Reichsführer of the *Schutzstaffeln*, the SS, the élite security corps initially formed to replace the SA, temporarily disbanded when the party was banned after the failed putsch. The first SS groups, formed in 1925, were individual units of no more than a dozen men whose role was to guard Hitler and other leading Nazis at rallies, defending them against possible assaults from leftist groups. Since then the units, now numbering about three hundred men overall, had become more cohesive. Part of Himmler's task was to form them into a single organisation nationwide.

The first orders he issued in his new role, on 17 September 1927, took immediate effect and provide intriguing evidence of his passion for detail. They were the regulations on how members of the corps should dress and conduct themselves in all aspects of their lives, on and off duty. The brightly coloured *Lederhosen* that many of them had formerly worn to stress their national identity were outlawed. Instead, their uniform featured dark and appropriately menacing hues: black cap, breeches, tie, boots and belt, with a brown shirt (later altered to white). Before every party meeting, SS guards had to parade for inspection, producing their party membership cards and even their party song books. Two singing practices, as well as two drill sessions, were to be scheduled each month.

SS men were forbidden to smoke while on duty at party meetings, or to leave while speeches were being made. Because their role was seen as military rather than political, they were not permitted to take part in the discussions. However, they were expected to report back to their superiors if they detected anything untoward or ideologically unsound during the proceedings. This was as important as their other intelligence role, to keep an eye on potential enemies, notably freemasons and Jewish leaders. Himmler, in his meticulous fashion, had the names, allegiances, views and personal details of suspected opponents entered in a carefully maintained card index file. In part, his vision of the role of the SS was based on reading books about the organisation of secret police forces by Napoleon and Stalin. In his 1990 biography of Himmler, Pater Padfield wrote:

> The SS was to be at once a secret police and a warrior élite, an instrument of internal conformity and a breeding ground for the purification of the race, the hammer of Jews, Slavs, communism and democracy and the agency for settling the east with Nordic farmers. It was to herald the Germanic millennium.

Although his role in the SS made increasing demands on his time, Himmler was able to take his mind off it long enough to get married. His bride was Margarete Boden, a divorcée eight years his senior. With her money they bought a smallholding where they bred and raised chickens and other livestock.

In January 1929 Himmler, who had been effectively in charge of the corps for some time, succeeded Erhard Heiden as *Reichsführer* of the SS. By the autumn of that year the SS had something like 5,000 members and would increase to an astonishing 40,000 by the summer of 1932. All the same, there had to be strict criteria for recruitment. Men must be at least 1.7m (5′7″) tall: Himmler himself just qualified at 1.75m. Above all, they must be, and be seen to be, of the correct racial stock. An applicant with Slavic looks would not do 'because he would very soon notice that he had no community of blood with his comrades of more Nordic origin'. That was why all applications to join had to be accompanied by photographs, which could be examined by the racial experts at headquarters.

A grading system for applicants was established. Initially they would be placed in one of five groups:

1. Pure Nordic
2. Predominantly Nordic
3. Light Alpine, with Dinaric (Mediterranean) additions
4. Predominantly eastern
5. Mongrels of non-European origin

Only men in the first three groups could be considered for SS membership. Once past that hurdle, they had to be graded for their physical attributes, on a scale of one to nine. Those rated four or better were admitted without question, seven or worse and they were rejected. Those in grades five and six were admitted if their enthusiasm made up for their physical inadequacy.

'In general,' said Himmler, 'we want only good fellows, not ruffians.' Probably to compensate for the fact that he would himself in all likelihood not have passed his own racial screening, he picked as his two senior aides men who epitomised the Aryan ideal – Reinhard Heydrich and Karl Wolff, both tall, blond, handsome and very obedient. He preferred men from the countryside – true Aryans, as he saw them – rather than the racially impure who dwelt in cities and corrupted those attracted there. He consistently sought to recruit young men from farming families. 'The best sons of the villages and later the best farmers must be members of this blood and life community of the SS,' he said in 1938.

This nostalgic, sentimental feeling that the Bavarian farmer was the salt of the earth was an integral part of the Nazi philosophy. Among the first laws passed in 1933 were the Hereditary Homestead Law and the Law for the New Formation of the German Farmerstock. These provided new homesteads and subsidies for farmers with the right racial credentials. The architect of these measures was Walther Darré, the Agriculture Minister, a race expert and friend of Himmler. The rural theme crops up throughout Himmler's life – manifesting itself, for instance, in the style of architecture he chose for the Lebensborn homes.

Himmler saw the SS as a racial élite of a very distinctive kind.

Joining members were told: 'The SS man is the most exemplary party member conceivable.' In a speech in 1934 Himmler described it as a 'knightly order, from which one cannot withdraw, to which one is recruited by blood and within which one remains with body and soul so long as one lives on this earth'. Hitler shared this vision. In 1941 he declared: 'I do not doubt for a moment that within 100 years or so from now all the German élite will be a product of the SS, for only the SS practises racial selection.'

Himmler was not a conventional Christian even in his youth. Although brought up a Catholic, he was expressing his doubts in his diary when he was only nineteen. 'I believe that I am coming into conflict with my religion,' he wrote in December 1919. 'Whatever may come, I will always love God, pray to him and remain attached to the Catholic church and defend it, even if I should be excluded from it.' His opposition to the established Church hardened as he became involved with the Nazis, and by 1933 he was sternly critical of it. The Christian concept of all men being equal under God obviously conflicted with the idea of a master race of superior beings. After reading Heinrich Bauer's *Children of the East* he noted in his book list: 'That is the tragedy of the Christian order, to fight against the valuable Prussians and then, faithlessly abandoned by the whole of Christianity and the clerics, to go under.'

In this he was influenced by Alfred Rosenberg, an Estonian who exerted an important influence on Nazi racial ideology. He wrote in 1932 that Christianity had 'tried to cripple the German soul' but 'today a new belief is awakening – belief in the blood and in defending the divine nature of man with the blood'. That belief 'replaces and overcomes the old sacrament'.

By 1937 Himmler's view was clear. 'We are living in a time of the final conflict with Christianity,' he wrote in *Plan for the Development of the German Heritage*. The Christian faith would be replaced by the 'development of the Germanic heritage', presenting 'the original picture of our forebears unspoilt and unchanged'. In the same year he wrote:

Whatever is Christian is not Germanic; whatever is Germanic is not Christian! Male pride, heroic courage and loyalty are Germanic; not gentleness, remorse, the misery of sin and a heaven with a prayer and psalms.

But he believed strongly that some form of faith, of loyalty to a greater cause, was vital. 'Only he who denies every belief in a higher force is godless to us,' he wrote in 1937. The creed that supplanted Christianity in his canon was a form of ancestor worship of early German heroes. 'How high, morally pure and sublime our forefathers were,' he wrote, after reading Tacitus's *Germania* in 1924. That was around the time he joined Artamen, a society formed by Dr Willibald Hentschell to promote a return to what he believed was the historic role of Germans as cultivators of the land, a pure-bred people of good looks, high intelligence and simple habits. Himmler soon moved to a position of authority in the society, as leader of its Bavarian section, and acted as a link between it and the Nazi Party.

In 1935, when he controlled virtually all the state security services, he founded a society of his own. The Ancestral Heritage Society was devoted to folk anthropology, examining the origins of Nordic families and races – 'the ancient, holy legacy'. His thesis was that the German race was older than Rome or Greece and had its own long-established cultural traditions, challenging the view that the Germans were barbarians until civilised by Christianity. He placed special significance on the runes, the letters of the early German alphabet. The SS symbol itself was based on one of them – the stylised S was the runic symbol of victory. The pierced V, representing life, became the badge of the *Lebensborn* homes. At one time Himmler advocated changing the names of the months to more traditional German terms: May, for instance, would have become *Wonnemond*, the month of ecstasy; August would be *Heurent*, the month for haymaking. Christmas would become the *Yulefest*, a traditional folk festival rather than a religious observance and the Christmas tree turned into the Yule tree.

His obsession with heroic myth emerged in a series of quasi-religious ceremonies he devised for the SS. The ceremony to mark the solstices involved lighting twelve candles. There were immutable rules about who should sit where and strictly enforced procedures for distributing the candles. At the appropriate time in the service, the congregation had to make these responses:

> We bow in reverence before the ancestors, whose blood, as mission and obligation, circulates in our veins.
> The brotherhood binds man to the duty of guarding his heritage.

The meaning of being is the unfolding of heritage into duty.

The family protects the sanctum in which the flame of life is kept.

Man and wife are donators, bearers and distributors of the germ of life.

We ourselves will become ancestors.

Our children are the witnesses of our breeding and of our being.

And our children will proclaim our greatness.

The naming ceremony for the children of SS men was similarly steeped in mumbo-jumbo. Uniformed men, ceremonial swords, the SS flag and a picture of Hitler on a central 'altar' decorated with swastikas, took the place of the more familiar furnishings of a church. The message 'Germany Awake' was displayed on a banner in large letters. The congregation was informed solemnly that 'National Socialism is an ideology that demands the whole man', and extracts from *Mein Kampf* were quoted instead of Bible readings.

The following blessing was then delivered by the 'priest' officiating at the ceremony:

> We believe in the god of all things
> And in the mission of our German blood,
> Which grows ever young from German soil.
> We believe in the race, carrier of the blood,
> And in the Führer, chosen for us by God.

The senior SS man present would then address the baby: 'We take you into our community as a limb of our body, you shall grow up in our protection and bring honour to your name, pride to your brotherhood and inextinguishable glory to your race.'

The formal entry procedures into the SS were also highly ritualistic, with key stages in the process timed to take place on important dates in the Nazi calendar. Young recruits from the Hitler Youth would be taken in on 9 November – the anniversary of the beer-hall putsch – to begin their training. On 30 January, the anniversary of Hitler being invited to form a government, they would be given their identity number. On 20 April, Hitler's birthday, they would swear their loyalty to the Führer and officially become candidate-entrants. There followed two and a half years of military, physical and ideological training of the strictest kind. In a speech in 1937 Himmler explained:

> I have set myself the practical exercise of extracting a new Germanic stem by means of selection according to appearance and by applying constant pressure, through a brutal selection procedure without human sentimentality, leading to the eradication of the weak and the unfit.

This was the survival of the fittest in its crudest form, the philosophy that every species has to fight for its very existence against ruthless competitors, with only the strong winning through. Hitler had spoken of creating 'a violent, fearless, cruel youth, from which the world will shrink in fear . . . It must bear pain. There can be nothing weak and tender in it.' Himmler explained:

> A process of selection is always something unmerciful and cruel, if you view it from our civilised standpoint. It is, however, logical and correct, as nature always is.

Yet for all his extreme views Himmler did not come across as a fanatic. Stephen Roberts, an Australian academic who visited Nazi Germany in 1937, wrote the following year that he was the most polite and hospitable of anyone in the Nazi hierarchy. 'Nobody I met in Germany is more normal.'

Those who survived the SS training were sworn into the order, again on the historic date of 9 November. They were handed their symbolic daggers and made to pledge that they and their families would abide by SS precepts. If they had not passed all the necessary tests by then they could try for the following two years before being pronounced unfit for admission to the élite.

Such a noble order needed a home base with appropriately chivalrous overtones, and at the end of 1933 Himmler came across the crumbling but romantic seventeenth-century castle of Wewelsburg in Westphalia, once occupied by the Bishops of Paderborn. It stands on a steep bluff and its round turrets with pointed roofs may have served as a model for the entrance tower Himmler later erected at the Lebensborn home at Steinhöring. He restored Wewelsburg expensively – using funds he had cajoled from big business and industry – and converted it not only into a school for SS members but more importantly into the knightly order's spiritual headquarters, the embodiment of its chivalrous virtues of moderation, constancy and loyalty.

In the large dining hall, in a deliberate echo of the English King Arthur, he installed a round table for seating his twelve senior 'knights', each of whom was assigned a coat of arms. In another room he created a memorial hall where, on the death of a 'knight', the body and his coat of arms would be cremated and the ashes placed in an urn to stand on one of the pillars that circled the room. For some of these ceremonies the men dressed up as medieval knights. Himmler also created a library of 12,000 books celebrating German greatness and the Aryan myth, to ensure that SS members saw themselves as members of a selected élite.

In doing all this, he was careful not to destroy the castle's original appearance, for architecture played an important part in his dream of creating a racially and culturally pure state. Not only would the new Germans share the flawless physical features and characteristics of their ancestors, but they would recreate ancient landscapes by putting up buildings in the historic Bavarian vernacular style. The *Lebensborn* homes were, where possible, located in traditional buildings and any extensions were designed along the same lines.

In January 1932 a 'Race Office' (RuSHA) was established at SS headquarters, headed by Walther Darré, an Argentine-born former chicken breeder – a profession Himmler had followed briefly – who was educated in Germany and England. Darré was author of a book called *Blood and Soil*, published by the Nazi Party in 1929. His thesis was that the German race was of exceptional quality, with blood as rich and fertile as the soil of the Fatherland on which these admirable people worked. They were a healthy breed who thrived in the countryside, unlike the decadent Jews and Slavs who preferred airless cities and whose blood was poisoning that of the true Germans. This is how he expressed his philosophy:

Just as we breed our Hanoverian horses using a few pure stallions and mares, so we will once again breed pure Nordic Germans by selective cross-breeding through the generations.

Perhaps we shall not be able to keep the whole of the German people pure through breeding, but the new German nobility will be pedigree in the literal sense of the word . . . From the human reservoir of the SS we shall breed a new nobility. We shall do it in a planned fashion and according to biological laws – as the noble-blooded of earlier times did instinctively.

Himmler was in total agreement, observing that it would be possible to 'attain the kind of success in the human sphere that one has had in the realm of animals and livestock'. At the same time he was conscious of the dangers of in-breeding: he was later to introduce a rule that at least a quarter of the annual SS intake should be men who were not the sons of existing members – and that the strict physical and intellectual criteria for admission should not be relaxed for SS men's sons.

As the central tool of the planned breeding programme, Darré's Race Office had set up a stringent selection process by which SS men and their wives had to trace their ancestry back through five generations, to before 1800. The first action of the office, confirmed on the very day it was established, was to promulgate strict rules controlling the marriage of SS men, to ensure that their hot-blooded instincts did not get the better of their duty to the future of the race. The ten-point Engagement and Marriage Decree, issued above Himmler's signature, stipulated:

1. The SS is an association of German men of Nordic determination selected on special criteria.
2. In conformity with the National Socialist creed, and recognising that the future of our people depends on the selection and retention of racially and hereditarily sound good blood, I establish with effect from 1 January 1932 the 'marriage consent' rule for all unmarried members of the SS.
3. The goal we strive for is an hereditarily sound and valuable clan of the German, Nordically-determined type.
4. Consent to marriage will be granted and denied solely and exclusively on the criteria of race and hereditary health.
5. Every SS man intending to marry must apply to the *Reichsführer-SS* for consent.
6. SS members who marry after having been denied consent will

be dismissed from the SS: they will be given the option of resigning.

7. Processing marriage requests is the task of the Race Office.

8. The Race Office manages the SS Clan Book, in which the families of SS members will be entered after the granting of marriage consent or the approval of a request for registration [of an existing marriage].

9. The *Reichsführer-SS*, the head of the Race Office and the specialists of this office are bound to secrecy on their word of honour.

10. The SS is clear that with this order it has taken a step of great significance. Derision, scorn and misunderstanding do not affect us. The future belongs to us.

If this remarkable document had been released to the outside world, derision and scorn would as like as not have been the initial responses – and there was something more than a little ludicrous about the procedures established to implement it. The bride- and groom-to-be were made to complete a long questionnaire concerning measurements of physical features, details of hair, eyes and skin colour, and as thorough a record as possible of the medical and racial background of themselves and their ancestors over the last 200 years. They also had to submit photographs of themselves in bathing costumes.

Himmler gave personal encouragement to his men to get down to their racial duty. In a high-spirited letter written in 1940 to Hermann Fegelein, a cavalry officer serving in Poland, he wrote:

The *Reichsführer-SS* does not want you to marry straight away in the former Poland, but he does expect you to make use of the lovely spring that is sure to follow this hard winter to make serious efforts to find a wife and to report your engagement to him by the end of May.

Yet derision would have been inappropriate, for the longer-term effect of the decree was far from humorous. It laid the foundations for the horrors of the ensuing decade, when Himmler's bizarre plan for the creation by selective breeding of a master race began to be put into practice. Its chief victims were the millions of Jews and others who died in concentration camps to make room for the new breed of supermen. But among others who have suffered, their lives irredeemably blighted, are those unlucky enough to have been born as a result of the Lebensborn experiment: Himmler's children.

3

Laying Down the Law

Should the Jew, with the help of his Marxist creed, conquer the
nations of this world, his crown will become the funeral wreath
of humanity, and once again this planet, empty of mankind, will
move through the ether as it did thousands of years ago.

Hitler in Mein Kampf

In January 1933, in the midst of political ferment provoked to a
significant extent by Nazi agitation, Hitler was asked by President
von Hindenburg to form a coalition government for Germany. The
following month came the Reichstag fire, staged by the SS to provoke
fears of a communist coup. It was used by Hitler as a pretext for the
Nazis to take absolute control of the machinery of the state and to
declare an emergency in which their opponents could be arrested
and imprisoned at will. Overnight *Mein Kampf* hitherto seen as no
more than a tendentious piece of extremist pamphleteering, became
the textbook for a political revolution, with anti-Semitism as its core
philosophy and its ultimate aim the creation of a Jew-free, Aryanised
Germany that would control a Jew-free, Aryanised empire covering
much of the world.

Himmler became chief of police in Munich. One of his first
acts in this new role was to establish a concentration camp at
a disused munitions factory at Dachau, just outside Munich, for
the incarceration of communist sympathisers and others thought
dangerous to the state, including many Jews. The prisoners were
forced to make elaborate shows of respect, reinforcing the SS guards'
image of themselves as an élite. Himmler drew up strict rules about
the exact style in which prisoners were to salute the guards and
he encouraged brutality as a means of confirming the distinction

between the wretches and their masters. An incorrect salute was punishable by fifty lashes of the whip and detention on a bread and water diet. The long list of offences that carried the death penalty for prisoners included disobedience and making a complaint.

His long-term aim was to create a national security force, totally loyal to Hitler, of which the SS would be a critical element. Hitler could see the value of such a force and let Himmler extend his empire virtually at will, until by early 1934 he had control of almost every police force and security organisation in the country except the Gestapo, the powerful secret police run from Berlin by the flamboyant Hermann Göring. By April the Gestapo, too, had entered Himmler's domain. He sold his Bavarian farm and moved to a villa in a Berlin suburb, to be close to the centre of power and influence. He took it upon himself to forge links with big business, whose financial support the party needed.

Yet he did not allow such worldly considerations to deflect him from his ideological purpose of purifying the German race – indeed, like Hitler, he saw them as steps towards it. From the moment they attained office the Nazis condoned anti-Semitic attacks by members of the SA, the unofficial paramilitaries who rounded up Jews at random and established camps for them – the so-called 'wild' camps – on disused factory sites. Very soon afterwards, the new government began remorselessly to turn Nazi racial theories into laws.

The first of them tackled what was seen as the most urgent problem, the elimination of Jews and other non-Aryans from positions of influence. The Law for the Restoration of the Professional Civil Service, passed in April – less than three months after Hitler became Chancellor – allowed for the dismissal from government service of anyone who was politically or racially undesirable; in other words communists and Jews.

In the same month came the law barring Jews from being doctors, dentists, teachers or students. Later the prohibition was broadened to include other occupations, including farming and the armed forces, and Jews were ousted from public insurance schemes. The following month saw the infamous book-burning, in which Jewish authors were specially targeted. It helped provoke the huge exodus of Jewish intellectuals, artists and scientists who were to enrich the cultural life and resources of other countries, especially the United States.

The Nazis were worried not only by racial impurities but also by inherited physical and mental flaws, as well as by the declining birthrate among healthy Germans. In 1929 Hitler had told a party rally at Nuremberg: 'If Germany was to get a million children a year and remove 700,000 to 800,000 of the weakest people, the final result might be an increase in strength.' In July 1933 the Sterilization Law was enacted, a key tool in the attempt to purify the race. It required doctors to register every case involving supposed hereditary illness which came to their notice, except in women over forty-five, and to recommend the sufferers for sterilization to prevent the illness from being passed on. The specified conditions included general feeble-mindedness, schizophrenia, manic depression, St Vitus's dance, epilepsy, hereditary blindness and deafness, serious physical deformities, and chronic alcoholism. Doctors who failed to register patients affected by these disabilities could incur a heavy fine.

The concept of feeble-mindedness included 'moral feeble-mindedness', a catch-all definition that could be used to cover any deviation from the social norm, such as promiscuity and homosexuality. (Another dictatorial regime, that of the Soviet Union, throughout its seventy-year history employed a technique of diagnosing nonconformists as mentally ill and confining them to institutions.)

Candidates for sterilisation would be compelled to appear before newly established Hereditary Health Courts, where doctors were 'obliged to testify without regard to professional confidentiality'. The courts used intelligence tests to measure suspected mental deficiencies. In their book *The Racial State* Michael Burleigh and Wolfgang Wippermann quote some sample questions. 'What day of the week is it? What type of state do we have at present? When is Christmas? Who discovered America? Why is there day and night? Why do children go to school?' The victims also had to make up sentences using three key words, including 'soldier ... war ... fatherland'.

Germany was not the only country to enact a sterilisation law. Indiana had introduced one as long ago as 1907 and it had been emulated by other American states. The American eugenicist Harry H. Laughlin was a great enthusiast and believed that his writings had in part inspired the German programme: in 1936 he was given an honorary doctorate at the University of Heidelberg. Denmark already had a similar law and so did parts of Switzerland, where a highly effective programme to control its gypsy population was not ended until 1972. Later in the 1930s sterilisation laws were passed in twelve more European and Latin American countries, but nowhere were they enforced as assiduously or on such a scale as in Germany, and nowhere else did they form a central strand of the ideology that governed the state.

In 1934, 181 Hereditary Health Courts were established, where a lawyer and two doctors decided in secret whether or not a person should be sterilised. In about 90 per cent of the cases they decided in favour of the operation and, although there was a right of appeal, the rulings were seldom reversed. (Later, when strict marriage controls were enacted, the courts' role was extended to deciding whether couples intending to marry were racially compatible.) Between 1 January 1934 and the start of the war five and a half years later, an estimated 320,000 Germans were sterilized – about half a per cent of the population. The preamble to the law explained:

> Since the National Revolution, public opinion has become increasingly pre-occupied with questions of demographic policy and the continuing decline in the birth rate. However, it is not only the decline in population which is a cause for serious concern but equally the increasingly evident genetic composition of our people. Whereas hereditarily healthy families have for the most part adopted a policy of having only one or two children, countless numbers of inferiors, and those suffering from hereditary conditions, are reproducing without restraint, allowing their sick and disadvantaged offspring to be a burden on the community.

In November this landmark legislation was supplemented by a law making castration mandatory for sex offenders. Other habitual criminals would have to submit to biological examination. An amendment added in 1935 introduced compulsory abortions during the first six months of pregnancy for women classified by the authorities as suffering from an hereditary illness. Euthanasia was to come later.

In 1935 the three so-called Nuremberg Laws were put into effect, 'to protect German blood and honour'. The first of them barred marriage and sexual relations between Jews and non-Jews, punishable by imprisonment (increased to death once the war had started).

However, people with only one Jewish grandparent out of the four were considered German and could marry non-Jews – although they could not, as we have seen, qualify to join the thoroughbred corps of the SS. Jews could not employ German servants aged under forty-five and were not allowed to fly the German national flag. Restrictions on Jews usually extended to other ethnic groups, especially gypsies and Negroes.

The second measure required all couples to submit to medical examination before marriage. If genetic illness was present in one of the partners the marriage was outlawed because it would involve 'racial damage', but if both partners were affected the marriage could go ahead after sterilisation. The effect of this law was wide-ranging, giving the authorities the power to choose precisely which couples the new German race was to be bred from.

Finally, the German people were divided into citizens and residents. A citizen had to be someone 'of German or related blood who through their behaviour make it evident that they are willing and able faithfully to serve the German people and nation'. Jews and unmarried women were merely residents and did not qualify for the privileges of citizenship – which included the right to vote.

Such rigid restrictions clearly required the establishment of strict procedures for ascertaining people's exact racial make-up. Anthropologists, biologists, racial hygienists, sociologists and historians were much in demand as institutions were set up to conduct the necessary research, and relatively few academics found that their scruples forbade them to participate in these challenging experiments. Such was the climate of the time that any overt disapproval of the Nazi way of doing things would have amounted to professional suicide. Like scientists developing deadly weapons, they could stifle any pangs of conscience by reminding themselves that, without a doubt, they were fulfilling the role of the scholar by extending the bounds of human knowledge, no matter to what political use their work was put.

Biology and medicine played key roles in Nazi ideology and medical imagery filled the party literature. At the Nuremberg party congress in 1929 a group of physicians formed the National Socialist League of German Physicians (NSDAB), aimed primarily at 'purifying' the profession by countering the influence of Jews and communists in it, but also encouraging discussion of such topics as sterilisation and euthanasia. About 13 per cent of German doctors then were Jewish, compared with a Jewish presence of about 1 per cent in the population as a whole. In Berlin, more than half the doctors were Jewish.

By the time Hitler came to power in 1933 the NSDAB had 2,786 members, but by that autumn the figure was 11,000 and soon the waiting list was so long that applications were temporarily suspended. Again, the motive for this rush to sign up was undoubtedly one of professional insurance. Jewish doctors were already being forced out: how long before the same happened to doctors thought to be less than enthusiasic Nazi supporters? With the rest of the German population rallying to the swastika, why should the doctors be any different?

In July 1934 a law was passed placing all public health matters under the direct control of the Nazi Party – an indication of their importance to the party creed. By 1943, membership of the NSDAB was 46,000; more than half the number of practising physicians. Addressing an early meeting of the League, Hitler said that although the revolution might survive without such professions as lawyers, engineers and builders, it would be lost without doctors: 'I cannot do without you for a single day, not a single hour. If you fail me, then all is lost.'

The leading medical journal, *Deutscher Arzteblatt*, espoused the Nazi cause enthusiastically, rejoicing in moves to purge medicine of outside influences and return to 'German feeling and German thinking'. An editorial in December 1933 declared: 'Never before has the German medical community been faced with such important tasks as those envisioned for it by the National Socialist ideal.' An example of the new medical and anthropological 'research' was an article in the journal *Nation and Race* by Dr Eugene Stahl from Stuttgart. He wrote that in determining racial characteristics it was not enough to look at the external shape of the body or even mental attributes:

We must go beyond this, to explore equally important differences in the inner organs of the body, differences that may reflect deeper physiological differences between the races. Best known in this area is 'racial smell'. Europeans find the smell not only of negroes but also of east Asians to be repulsive, even when they are clean. The Oriental himself will of course make similar claims.

From 1933, courses in racial hygiene were offered to all medical students and there was growing pressure to enrol in them. That autumn the State Medical Academy in Berlin offered its first courses on the subject. The German Society for Racial Hygiene was established in 1933, and in 1937 the existing German Society for Anthropology was renamed the German Society for Racial Research. The Kaiser Wilhelm Institute for Anthropology, Heredity and Eugenics was the most influential and active of the research bodies. It was here that Dr Josef Mengele, the physician at Auschwitz concentration camp during the war, sent the eyes of murdered gypsies, the internal organs of children and other material that could be analysed for identifiable hereditary factors. He was obsessed with genetics and heredity and committed to the idea of improving the stock through selective breeding.

These and other academic bodies received government funds so long as their work was connected with the creation of the new racial Utopia. Their advice was sought on whether an individual was or was not an authentic Aryan and whether a particular disease was hereditary. Training courses were offered on how to research family history so as to determine whether a couple's ancestry was sufficiently pure to allow them to obtain a certificate to marry.

In 1933 the Interior Ministry appointed leading scientists from these societies to its new Committee of Experts on Population and Racial Policy, of which Himmler and Darré were also members. At the committee's first meeting the Interior Minister, Dr Wilhelm Frick, laid down the guidelines for population policy. It was, he said, the racial duty of healthy Germans to have children, not a matter of personal choice. He advocated a return to large peasant families, so as to reunite Nordic blood with the soil. At the same time hereditarily defective people must be prevented from having children, and racially mixed marriages must be outlawed.

Himmler further increased his power after the bloody 'Night of the Long Knives' in June 1934. His old mentor Röhm was the chief victim of the purge, carried out by Himmler's SS, which left more than two hundred senior Nazis dead and consolidated Hitler's position as party leader. Röhm was leader of the SA, the unofficial army that had been a vital instrument in the Nazis' rise to power. It was still larger than the SS and Gestapo but it was becoming an increasing embarrassment to the leadership because it was hard to control. Donations to its coffers were extorted through menaces and its officer corps was notorious for drunkenness, homosexuality and degeneracy – scarcely a good example for what was supposed to be a morally and racially pure state.

When the SA was in effect the Nazis' only street weapon these excesses were tolerated because they were an inherent part of the unreasoning image that provoked terror in their enemies and persuaded other Germans that it was simpler and safer to humour Hitler than to confront him. Now that the party was in power it had more formal and reliable means of coercion at its disposal. So long as he could rely on the loyalty of the professional army, Hitler had no further need of the SA – of which, for obvious reasons, the regular armed services greatly disapproved.

Although he had a lingering sense that he owed a debt of loyalty to Röhm, Hitler was persuaded to act by Himmler and Göring – still powerful despite losing overall control of the Gestapo – who were determined that their old colleague must be eliminated. In his methodical way, Himmler had made a neat list of people who, in his view, could not be relied upon, or who constituted a possible threat to his own position. He called it the 'Reich List of Unwanted Persons' and it even included Gregor Strasser, the man who had given him his first party post.

It is impossible to judge just how far Himmler was motivated by personal rivalries and ambition and how far by the genuine political and philosophical differences that divided him from Röhm and his allies. The SA leaders were advocates of a populist revolution that would sweep away the landed gentry and their hereditary privileges. Himmler, the traditionalist, was decidedly of the other faction, which wanted to preserve the old social order but to superimpose the Nazi state on to it – the course that was eventually followed.

In the paranoic atmosphere of the time, Himmler and Göring did not find it hard to persuade Hitler that Röhm, Strasser and the others on the list were plotting against him. Hitler himself flew to Bavaria to place Röhm under arrest on 30 June and to order his execution two days later. Himmler and Göring, who had been simultaneously taking care of Hitler's 'enemies' in Berlin, were among the group of loyal lieutenants who solemnly welcomed the Führer back at Tempelhof airport after his deadly mission. After two days the executions ceased, the victims were cremated and their ashes returned to their families.

That October, Himmler explained to Gestapo chiefs why the purge had been carried out, why he and the others had to 'shoot one's own comrades, with whom one has stood side by side for eight or ten years in the struggle for an ideal and who had then failed'. He blamed it on Jews, freemasons and Catholics, who had 'sent numerous individuals into the SA and the entourage of the former Chief of Staff and drove him to catastrophe'. Had the action not been taken, he maintained, chaos would have ensued, giving 'a foreign enemy' the pretext for marching in and assuming control of Germany.

Meanwhile, in the Provincial Race Office in Jena, south-west of Leipzig, Himmler was looking into another aspect of heredity and racial hygiene. He commissioned a large research project on whether homosexuality was inherited, and whether it could be 'cured' by hormone implants. (Much later, during the war, a Danish doctor named Carl Vaernet carried out more extensive experiments on homosexual prisoners at Buchenwald, and claimed to have found a way of reversing their homosexuality by administering hormones.)

The presence of Röhm, an overt homosexual, in the party hierarchy had given this particular minority group a measure of protection against persecution, but since his liquidation they had become as vulnerable as any of the others. Himmler resented homosexuals of sound Aryan stock not so much on moral grounds but because they represented a waste of breeding material. In 1935 he established a central register of homosexuals and the following year created the Reich Central Office for Combatting Homosexuality and Abortion. In 1936 more than 4,000 men were imprisoned for homosexual acts, compared with only 766 in 1934. After their release from prison, many were sent to concentration camps, where they were forced to wear pink triangles on their clothing.

But Jews remained the primary target. The most vicious anti-Semitic legislation was enacted in 1938, in a series of measures announced remorselessly month after month, having the cumulative effect of, by stages, squeezing Jews out of any meaningful participation in the life of the state. The laws included:

- a ban on changing names, with Jews specifically barred from taking German names;
- an ordinance designating 316 names as officially Jewish: Jews with other names had to add 'Israel' or 'Sarah' to avoid misunderstanding;
- Aryan parents must not give their children any of the Jewish names;
- Jewish businesses must not conceal their ownership;
- all Jewish organisations must register with the authorities;
- all Jewish property and assets to be registered;
- Jews must carry papers showing them to be Jewish, and show the documents when asked;
- all streets named after Jews to have new names;
- Jews not allowed to act as estate agents, money-lenders, factory managers, detectives, tourist guides, marriage brokers, nurses, midwives, arms dealers or travelling salesman. They could not run mail-order business or work in public markets or mortuaries;
- Jewish physicians only allowed to treat other Jews, and then only with special permission;
- Jews barred from German theatres;
- Jewish children expelled from German schools;
- Jews confined to specified residential areas.

In 1941 the law was passed that required all Jews to display the Star of David. From there it was only a short step to the Final Solution.

After the 1934 purge, the Nazi leadership was not again seriously contested until the latter stages of the Second World War. Having crushed what he believed to be internal enemies – and more importantly conveyed a powerful warning to any who might think of challenging him in the future – Hitler was free to build up the armies that would enable him to enforce his vision of the Aryan Utopia spreading across Europe.

As for Himmler, his biographer Peter Padfield maintains that the murders of 30 June 1934 marked his emergence as 'power broker of the Third Reich'. More important than that, his new status allowed him to pursue his most treasured project, the programme for improving the breed of future citizens of the Thousand Year

Reich, while eliminating those deemed unworthy to live in it. His SS was to be the instrument for both strands of the policy. The *Lebensborn* homes, the most far-reaching element of the programme, got under way in 1935.

4

A Matter of Breeding

It is clear that those of our people with less valuable blood always mature earlier than our own intrinsic type. They are always more engaging and more compliant sexually than our type and for that reason they get their man. Now comes the change. I believe we have an era before us when the Nordic girl will marry and the other remain on the shelf.

Heinrich Himmler, 1936

In January 1926 Himmler read a book called *Germany's Vanishing People* by Dr A. Thomsen. It worried him, as he confided in his reading list: 'The awful thing in Germany today is that women no longer want to become mothers. May God put this situation to rights.' The statistics bore this out dramatically. At the beginning of the century the German annual birthrate was a healthy 33 per thousand population. By the 1920s it was down to 20.3 and by 1933 only 14.7 – less than half the rate a mere three decades earlier.

Himmler continued to be troubled throughout his life by this dereliction of duty, as he saw it, in the nation's women. In a speech to SS group leaders in Tolz in 1937 he declared that a nation with many children could become a world power, while a barren nation was on its way to the grave. 'A nation that reveres its ancestors always has children and thus has eternal life.' During the war he told SS volunteers in Norway: 'A man can die peacefully when he has sons.'

To the Nazi ideologues, motherhood was the only proper role for a woman, while fatherhood was something a man could take care of when not fulfilling life's other pressing functions. As early as 1921, the party published a declaration of principle to the effect that women should be excluded from major political office, but Hitler was keen to stress that this did not mean that their role was insignificant. 'In my state', he said on 8 September 1934, 'the mother is the most important citizen.' In his ideal Aryan world the strong, blond men were the warriors and leaders, while their lithe and equally healthy women stayed at home to fulfil the function that biology had allotted them. This attitude was in part dictated by the racial imperative and was linked with his concerns about the falling birthrate among Aryans. It also did him no harm electorally, gaining him support from traditionalist sections of German society.

Dr Josef Goebbels, the party's propaganda chief, reinforced the argument. 'A woman's duty is to be attractive and bear children,' he wrote. 'The idea is not as crude and old-fashioned as it may seem. A female bird makes herself desirable to her mate and sits on her eggs for him. To remove women from public life is to restore their feminine dignity.' His propaganda machinery was put at the disposal of the breeding campaign. Lyrical posters went up emphasising the virtues of motherhood, illustrated by a child suckling at a pure Aryan breast – an image closely linked to the statue at Steinhöring. Propaganda films, shown in all cinemas by decree, delivered the same message and underlined the falling birth statistics. Other films addressed different aspects of the racial question: the dangers of hereditary illness, the advantages of euthanasia and, the all-time favourite, the international Jewish conspiracy, culminating in the notorious film that depicted Jews as rats.

Even standard manuals about health and motherhood adopted a hectoring and evangelical tone. In *The German Mother and Her First Child*, published just before the war, Dr Johanna Haarer wrote of a woman's transcendental duty to bear issue:

> At all periods of history, becoming a mother has been compared with the highest virtue of man who, in the most dire moments of need, stakes his life for the country and the people . . . Today we are experiencing a great campaign led by the leadership of the state by which the genetically healthy and the racially valuable must be defended against all that is sick and decadent and which is allowed to blossom under a falsely understood concept of freedom.

Alongside the tools of persuasion, concrete measures were devised to encourage women to fulfil their perceived duty. Mothers of three or more children under ten years old were given 'honour cards' entitling them to jump queues in shops, and local authorities allowed them rebates on rent and public utility bills. Loans, funded by extra taxes on single people, were awarded to young couples to help them set up home, if they had the proper racial credentials. With each child born, a quarter of the loan was cancelled – so after the birth of the fourth all repayments would cease.

Initially a condition of the loans was that the women gave up work. To further discourage them from working, quotas were introduced for higher education; only 10 per cent of students could be female and all of these had to study needlework as part of their courses. A low ceiling was placed on the number of women entering the learned professions. Many of these regulations were dropped as war approached and women were needed to replace fighting men in the factories and elsewhere, until eventually the labour shortage grew so severe that foreign women were recruited.

The perception of woman as housewife was not so rigid, however, as to bar her from political activity of the approved kind. Women were encouraged to be active in party organisations, chiefly National Socialist Womanhood (NSF), which by 1938 had 2.3 million members. In 1934 the NSF chose as its leader a woman who was the model of patriotic virtue – Gertrud Scholtz-Klink, mother of eleven children. Few were better qualified to be awarded the Honour Cross of the German Mother, introduced in 1938 for mothers of large families. (One of its more dubious benefits was that members of the Hitler Youth were required to salute recipients of it in public.)

Those were the carrots. The stick was a two-year prison sentence on anyone carrying out an abortion on an Aryan woman without an overwhelming medical reason; the penalty was increased to death after the war started. The supply of contraceptives was strictly controlled and groups advocating birth control were suppressed. Abortions for non-Aryans, or German women bearing the children of undesirable foreigners, were, by contrast, encouraged. An easing of the divorce law in 1938 was aimed at freeing couples to marry again and produce children. Where previously adultery had been the only grounds for a divorce, it was now possible to obtain one if your spouse had refused to conceive a child, had an abortion or had been living apart from you for three years.

Himmler was ambivalent about marriage. According to his chiropractitioner, Felix Kersten, whose memoirs of his discussions with Himmler are by far the most revealing source of information about the *Reichsführer*, he was planning after the war to release senior Nazis and SS men from their existing marriages (to 'good honest housewives') and mate them with specially selected young women trained in his proposed 'Women's High Schools for Wisdom and Culture'. Characteristically, he purported to have found a historical precedent for this in the 'wise women' of the ancient German people and the vestal virgins of Rome. He believed that the decline in the quality of the stock of modern German nobility was caused by paying too little regard to the racial quality of their spouses. Himmler abided by his own libertarian principles: he had a daughter by his wife, Margarete, and two sons by his young mistress, Hedwig Potthast.

Until the new plan could be implemented, marriage was not regarded as a prerequisite for contributing to the increase in population. The children of single women, if their pedigree measured up, were just as valuable to the Reich. In October 1939, just after the war began, Himmler issued an order to the SS in which he declared:

> The greatest gift for the widow of a man who falls in battle is always the child of the man she loved. But beyond the scope of bourgeois laws and customs – which are otherwise no doubt necessary – it can be an exalted duty for German women of good blood, even outside marriage, to bear children to soldiers called to war who may not return. This is not a trivial task, but one that should be undertaken deliberately and seriously.

He went on to promise that the SS would look after the welfare of the children and their mothers, whether married or not, in cases where the father was killed.

The trouble was that most twentieth-century Germans were by nature conservative and their perception of single mothers and their children was stubbornly disapproving – an attitude encouraged by the Church. There was a clash between the Nazi concept of moral order and the Germanic virtues on the one hand, and on the other the libertinism inherent in breeding out of wedlock; a contradiction that the Lebensborn organisation was never quite able to resolve. Dr Gregor Ebner, the first chief medical officer for the Lebensborn homes, felt obliged in 1937 to defend the practice of catering for the children of unmarried as well as of married women. Admitting that this went against 'the usual liberal bourgeois and church dogma,' he wrote:

They accuse us of undermining the institution of marriage – the underpinning of the National Socialist State – and say that legitimate children should be given the best care of all. We agree that marriage is the best possible situation if they are pure-bred German men and women but we also know that many young men and women are not in a position to get married. Should the children of such parents be treated as inferior? Or do we want, as good national socialists, to reject these bourgeois attitudes and replace them with a standard of worth that relates to the good blood needed by our race? These mothers are just the same as other mothers at the moment when they first set eyes on their beautiful little babies and hear their first cry. We can't preach morals about these things. What helps the race is good and what harms the race is bad.

Himmler pleaded similarly compassionate motives. In a speech at Kochem he declared: 'I do not find it right that some poor young girl expecting an illegitimate child is rejected by everyone when she has only done what her nature demanded.'

In an effort to remove the stigma attached to unmarried mothers, the Ministry of Justice decreed in 1937 that they could call themselves 'Frau' – a term hitherto reserved for married women. More propaganda leaflets were issued, arguing against blanket condemnation of illegitimacy. In 1939 the ban on single mothers in the civil service was lifted.

In his *Social History of the Third Reich*, Richard Grunberger commented:

The Third Reich did manage to inculcate new notions about the sexual role of women in society. Most previous arrangements of society had been characterised by the advantage men enjoyed over women in the sexual sphere, an advantage exemplified by what is known as the double standard of morality. The Third Reich replaced the conventional double standard of bourgeois society by immorality pure and simple, and the sexual role of women by their biological one.

This belief in motherhood as a separate institution from marriage, and in the primary duty of women to fulfil their biological function regardless of emotional involvement, lay at the root of the Lebensborn concept. It was all part of the central Nazi belief that individual feelings and preferences must be subordinated to the needs of the state, for the ultimate victory and the attainment of the new, racially pure world order.

The Lebensborn organisation was decidedly Himmler's baby. It was founded on 12 December 1935, the year he established the Ancestral Heritage Society (Ahnenerbe) for the purpose of proving scientifically the superiority of the Nordic races. The link was clear: the Ahnenerbe was to provide theoretical justification for the racial breeding that was the purpose of the Lebensborn homes.

On 13 September 1936, nine months after setting up the organisation, Himmler brought it under the direct aegis of the SS. It was a logical move, given that he had identified this élite, hand-picked corps as the chief instrument for his breeding programme, the prime begetter of the new Aryan nation.

The despicable acts of SS guards at concentration camps have led to the SS being viewed generally as little more than a gang of sadistic thugs. Yet the corps represented a great deal more than that, embodying much else that was most sinister in Nazi philosophy. Himmler saw it as a knightly order, with its own flame-lit initiation ceremony, its oath ('Obedience unto death'), its ceremonial swords and insignia and its headquarters in a medieval Westphalian castle. He commemorated the SS's assumption of control over Lebensborn by setting out what he expected from his élite force in the field of paternity:

A marriage with few children is little more than an affair. I hope members of the SS, and especially its leaders, will set a good example. Four children is the minimum necessary for a good and healthy marriage. In the event of childlessness it is the duty of every SS leader to adopt racially valuable children, free of hereditary illnesses, and inculcate them with the spirit of our philosophy . . . The Lebensborn organisation will aid SS leaders in the selection and adoption of racially valuable children.

In a later speech he became even more demanding, requiring that SS men should produce not merely four children but four sons. He explained how he arrived at this critical figure: it allowed two of them to be killed in battle, leaving two to continue the bloodline: 'The leadership of a nation having one son or two per family will have to be fainthearted . . . They will have to tell themselves: "We cannot afford it."'

Himmler outlined the aims of Lebensborn unequivocally, in these terms:

1. To support large families that are racially and genetically valuable.
2. To look after expectant mothers who are racially and genetically valuable and who, after careful research by the Race and Settlement Head Office into their families and the families of their children's fathers, can be expected to give birth to equally valuable children.
3. To care for such children.
4. To care for the mothers after the children are born.

Care and support: carefully chosen words to create an image of a totally benign welfare organisation. That was certainly how the leading officials of Lebensborn sought to project it at the Nuremberg trials after the war and at their separate trial in Munich in 1950. And such, in its own very limited way, it was. The mothers of illegitimate children, who might otherwise have had nowhere to turn for practical help and sympathy, could find a refuge here – as long as they had taken the elementary precaution of ensuring their lover's racial purity as well as their own, and of being able to establish their blood-lines with sufficient certainty to satisfy the demanding criteria of the authorities.

Although unmarried women were the chief beneficiaries, married women were taken in as well – either because their child was not fathered by their husband, or simply because they wanted to take advantage of the unusually high standard of medical and nursing care. Marital status was irrelevant. It mattered only that the prospective parents were racially pure.

The chief attraction of the homes, as far as the mothers were concerned, was that their responsibility for their children could, if they wished, be taken entirely off their hands almost immediately after the birth. All children in the homes became in effect the property of the SS. The mothers could, with permission, take them away and bring them up themselves – which many of the married women and a few of the single ..others did. The SS would make sure that the natural fathers supported their children, even if their paternity was not acknowledged publicly.

In those cases where the mothers did not want to keep their children, as most did not, the SS took responsibility for placing them in politically correct (which meant devotedly Nazi) families, selected with great care and attention to detail, as with the best adoption agencies today. 'In this way,' Ebner wrote, 'later generations of racially valuable children will best be protected.'

Every effort was made to ensure secrecy and thus avoid embarrassment or shame. Doctors at the homes were made to sign an SS oath of silence and to 'respect the honour of pregnant women, whether they conceived before marriage or after.' Taking photographs of the mothers was forbidden: pictures that have survived from the homes are nearly all of the babies, the nurses, the buildings and the gardens.

The homes had their own procedures for registering births, bypassing the official civic registries. Illegitimate children were not described as such on official documents: they were provided with simple certificates confirming their racial purity to avoid problems with the bureaucracy later in their lives. This is one reason why today the German children born in the homes are virtually impossible to trace.

From the start the Lebensborn organisation had its headquarters in Munich, Himmler's power base. Himmler would personally scour the countryside, looking for suitable premises and locations for the homes. Steinhöring, less than an hour's drive from Munich, was an obvious place for the first one, given Himmler's requirement that they should be away from polluted cities. The building that became the Hochland home formerly belonged to the Catholic

Church, which had used it as a hostel for retired priests and then as a children's home. It was bought by the Bavarian State Government for RM55,000. Himmler spent RM540,000 on making it suitable for its new purpose and had it embellished with symbols appropriate to his philosophy – a tall watchtower like the turret of a medieval castle, iron gates bearing runic symbols and the stylised initials SS.

An important influence on Himmler's thinking about heredity was Dr Gregor Ebner, whom he first knew when they were at university in Munich together. Born in 1892, Ebner, a general practitioner in a Munich suburb, joined the Nazi Party in 1930 and soon became an official of his local branch. He went into the SS the following year and gave lectures to members about racial selection and health. This was when his acquaintance with Himmler grew into a close family friendship. It seems certain that Himmler consulted Ebner at every stage of the development of the Lebensborn idea, and in 1936 he appointed him medical consultant for the Hochland home in Steinhöring. The following year Ebner gave up his private practice and was appointed chief medical officer for all the homes. Since the term 'medical' embraced every aspect of racial selection he was the most important person in the hierarchy, reporting direct to Himmler.

On his appointment, Ebner set out his philosophy in a wide-ranging essay. He wrote:

The German future stands or falls with the German child. It follows that the start of finding a solution to the [population] problem is in the way people are advised about marriage, in particular their choice of suitable partners. It is a rule handed down from God that the worth of each person in his own right has been inherited from his ancestors. A child cannot be made into a racially valuable person by the way it is brought up. That is why the National Socialist state makes a priority of selecting with care, as a matter of duty, those who are racially and hereditarily valuable.

Ebner stressed again and again that whether or not the child's parents were married was not a significant question:

The illegitimate child must not be allowed to suffer from the fact that in today's circumstances it is sadly not possible for many young fathers and mothers to get married ... Any mother of an illegitimate child who is prepared to give life to a child will also be supported by Lebensborn. In these mother-and-baby homes a mother can, free from the cares of daily life, have her child in peace. The best sort of care will be given: doctors, large rooms full of sun and light, wonderful cleanliness and a beautiful landscaped environment to make it easier for a mother going through one of her most difficult times ... Life in the homes is not meant to be like life in a clinic but like living in a family group. No class distinction is made: it is genuine communal living.

In 1939, two years after he joined the organisation, Ebner gave a progress report. By then six homes were operating: Hochland at Steinhöring; Hohehorst (hilltop) near Bremen; the Harz home at Wernigerode, south of Brunswick; Kurmark at Klosterheide, north of Berlin; Bad Polzin in Poland; and Wienerwald near Vienna. There were now 263 beds for mothers and 487 for children available.

By the end of 1938, the number of mothers admitted was 653. More than twice as many had applied for admission but Ebner reported that, after the strict racial tests had been carried out, only 40 per cent of parents were found to have come from sufficiently pure racial stock to qualify. He claimed that infant mortality was only half as high in the homes as in the rest of Germany – 3 per cent as against 6 per cent. 'The births are very easy, without many complications. This is attributable to the racial selection and the quality of women we get.'

However, although that quality did not noticeably decline, the infant mortality rate increased worryingly from about the time the war began. The trend was upwards throughout 1940, as it was in the rest of Germany, and by the end of the year the rate was up by almost half to 4.23 per cent. Ebner thought that this may have been because the mothers were leaving the homes too early – usually four to six weeks after the birth – and were thus not breast-feeding their babies for long enough: both he and Himmler placed considerable importance on breast-feeding. He therefore increased to four months the recommended time for the mothers to stay, even though that would have seriously reduced the numbers the homes could accommodate.

In the event most mothers, especially those who had decided to give their children up for adoption, left in less than two months. The infant mortality rate did fall a little but would never again get back as low as 3 per cent. (In 1943 the increasing pressure on the homes, caused by the desire for more births to replace men lost in the fighting, led to a reversal in policy and mothers were made to leave after a fortnight.)

In his 1939 report, Ebner gave some details of the finances of the operation. The cost of keeping a mother there to have her baby was RM400, 'but that isn't much of a sacrifice if you can save a thousand children of good blood'. He added that RM3,000 was being paid out to 110 families of SS men, based on the number of children in them. Money was raised in many ways. There was a levy on members of the Lebensborn Society. The society had 13,000 members at the time of Ebner's report, of which 8,000 belonged to the SS (membership was compulsory for senior officers) and 766 to various branches of the police. By the end of the war membership had reached 17,000.

The levy was at least RM27 a month, but it went up for those SS contributors who were failing in their paternal duties. Those who had fathered no children by the age of twenty-eight had to pay more, and the compulsory levy went up again at thirty unless they had at least two children by then. The 'fines' grew stiffer as the men grew older without fulfilling their norm. In addition, they would find their path to promotion blocked if they had not displayed appropriate fecundity. The leaflet outlining these rules for the benefit of SS members contained this wry comment:

> Those who think they can escape their obligations to the nation and the race by remaining unmarried will pay subscriptions at a level that will persuade them to prefer the married to the single state.

The fathers of the children, whether married or not, were also required to contribute to the homes, and the mothers had to hand over their health and social security payments.

The money thus raised was, however, nothing like enough to meet the needs of the expanding Lebensborn organisation. In 1939 the

Finance Ministry gave a grant of RM1 million to offset a growing deficit. The large capital sums needed to buy and equip the homes came through the NS-Volkswohlfahrt or NSV, the National Socialist People's Welfare Organisation – which was later to compete with the Lebensborns for primacy in the fields of child care and adoption. In the early thirties the NSV raised a large part of its funds from coercive street collections and it had a 'Mother and Child Relief' section even before the establishment of the Lebensborns, as well as its better-known 'Winter Relief' programme. It was by no means a conventional welfare organisation that gave help where the need was greatest, as Josef Goebbels, the head of Nazi propaganda, made clear in a speech in 1938:

> Our starting point is not the individual and we do not accept the view that one should feed the hungry, give drink to the thirsty or clothe the naked. Our objectives are completely different. They can be summed up neatly in one sentence: we must have a healthy people so as to triumph in the world.

After the SS took over the Lebensborn homes, capital funding came from different sources, partly from the donations of Himmler's friends in the business community and partly from assets seized from Jews. The homes were often sited in what had once been Jewish-run clinics or sanatoriums; the administrative headquarters of Lebensborn in Munich was formerly the office of a Jewish communal organisation.

Jewish property was also exploited in other ways. In 1942 Ebner wrote to the Mayor of the Bavarian town of Ichenhausen, asking for a favour. Stressing that the Lebensborn homes were a pet project of Himmler's, he said that one of the mothers at Steinhöring was looking for somewhere to live.

> Since I have heard from my sister that in Ichenhausen a lot of Jewish families have been evacuated, there isn't the housing problem that there is here. Here [in Munich] I have been able to get hold of many apartments that once belonged to Jewish families. I should be delighted to be able to report to the *Reichsführer* that people like you are giving full support to his work on the population problem.

In 1936 Himmler appointed Dr Guntram Pflaum, a senior SS officer and former salesman, to administer the organisation, although Dr Ebner was in charge of the all-important medical aspects, including decisions on whether parents were sufficiently Aryan to justify a place in a home. In 1940 Pflaum, who had clashed with Himmler after allegations of financial mismanagement, was replaced by Max Sollmann, a Himmler confidant. Born in 1904, Sollmann had joined the Nazi Party at the age of eighteen and a year later took part with Himmler in the Munich beer-hall putsch. For some years he worked for German companies in Colombia but returned to Germany in 1934 and joined the SS in 1937.

Sollmann reorganised the command structure of Lebensborn so that power was effectively shared between him and Ebner, both reporting to Himmler. Greater centralisation of authority was reflected in the rapid increase in headquarters staff, from twenty-three at the end of 1937 to 220 by the beginning of 1942.

With the change in the administration of the homes, Himmler's personal involvement grew. He took a strong interest in all the fine detail, especially the medical and dietary aspects. Occasionally this verged on obsession, as in a memo urging that the mothers should be persuaded to eat porridge, which he had identified as a vital factor in forming the sterling racial qualities of the British ruling class – an élite group that he admired greatly. He dismissed the mothers' fears that porridge was fattening by pointing to the slender figure of Lord Halifax, the British Foreign Secretary: proof, as he saw it, that the creamy oats 'have no influence on the weight of people of quality'.

He insisted that cooks be instructed in the correct steaming of vegetables to maximise their nutritional value; that potatoes should be served in their skins and wholemeal bread provided where possible. He also recommended fresh salads and sunflower seeds and insisted that the mothers, despite their protests, should be given regular doses of castor oil. Until the very end of the war, he ensured that the homes had priority in the distribution of luxuries such as fresh fruit, which became increasingly scarce.

The furnishings and upholstery in the homes were the best that his considerable influence could obtain from those looted from Jewish residences and institutions. For such items the home had its own supply chain, in which the railway from the Dachau concentration camp was an important link. Stories abound of loot being brought up from Dachau and unloaded by prisoners, who also provided a pool of free labour to extend and improve the homes. A squad of about thirty Dachau prisoners, mostly Poles, was assigned to the organisation, but the men were strictly forbidden to make any contact with the mothers. The heavy domestic work was done by female prisoners, some of them Jehovah's Witnesses who had been confined at Ravensbrück. 'It was a good life,' one Lebensborn mother recollects. 'And the childcare was excellent.'

Although Germany was engaged in a war whose prosecution demanded sacrifices from everyone, Himmler believed that the Lebensborn project was just as important as the war effort – indeed, that the two crusades were virtually inextricable, since one could not be said to have fulfilled its ultimate purpose unless the other had as well.

The Second World War was essentially a racial war, aimed at creating space for a purified German race at the expense of the 'inferior' Slavs, Jews and Mediterranean peoples. Some analysts believe that this explains why Hitler did not invade Britain after the fall of France in 1940, because he saw the British as primarily a Germanic people. Himmler repeatedly told Felix Kersten that Hitler's vision was of a world hegemony shared by Germany and Britain, with the British navy controlling the seas and the German army the land. (Hitler admired Britain's imperial record, and his attempts to colonise the eastern lands was partly based on it.) Himmler believed that the British people would favour such a solution, but felt that the ruling class was so much under the influence of the Jews that it was blind to the advantages of this arrangement. The direct link between the Lebensborn project and the war effort was explained by Himmler in this letter to Field-Marshal Wilhelm Keitel:

According to statistics there are 600,000 abortions a year in Germany. The fact that these happen among the best German racial types has been worrying me for years. The way I see it we cannot afford to lose these young people, hundreds and thousands of them. The aim of protecting this German blood is of the highest priority. If we manage to stop these abortions we will be able to have 200 more German regiments every year on the march. Another 500,000 to 600,000 people could produce millions of marks for the economy. The strength of these soldiers and workers will build the greater Germany. This is why I founded Lebensborn in 1936. It fights abortions in a positive way. Every woman can have her child in peace and quiet and devote her life to the betterment of the race.

The theme of peace, quiet and comfort recurs constantly in Himmler's recorded references to Lebensborn. Pampering the mothers with good food and fine furnishings was part of the strategy of convincing them that there was no stigma attached to their position, and that on the contrary their contribution to the state was greatly valued. They were encouraged to look on their stay as a kind of working holiday: a range of postcards, showing views of the home, was available for them to send to their families and lovers.

The official brochure about the homes, issued to prospective mothers, was so tasteful that it could almost have been a promotion leaflet for a chain of luxury country hotels or health farms, with photographs of the homes carefully shot to underline their rural and restful attributes. But there were differences. At the front was the three-pronged Lebensborn symbol, based on ancient German runes, emerging from the Nazi swastika. The title page bore the message 'It is sacred to be a mother of good blood', and opposite was a picture of a blonde and wholesome young woman.

Himmler elaborated on the principle to Kersten:

My first aim in setting up the Lebensborn was to meet a crying need to give unmarried women, who were racially pure, the chance to have their children free of cost. There they could pass the weeks before the birth of their child in agreeable surroundings and quietly await the great event. You can hardly realize how much it means to a woman, who used to be cold-shouldered and insulted because her child was illegitimate, to enter a home where she can relax spiritually and physically, receive medical attention and feel that everybody is glad about the child she's going to have.

While Himmler regarded the physical well-being of the mothers as all-important, their political welfare was not neglected either. In the early days courses had been devised to make the women into even better Nazis than they were when they arrived. Typically, the mothers had to attend three classroom sessions of ideological instruction a week. They were shown propaganda films, exposed to radio lectures and made to sing communal party songs. Some of the women resented this and complained. Before the war, local party officials would visit the schools to help with the classes, although these visits were abandoned when the conflict began because of other demands on the party workers' time.

Children born on Himmler's birthday, 7 October, received special privileges. At birth they were given a candlestick (made to order in the Dachau concentration camp) and at every birthday they were sent one candle for every year of their age and the gift of one mark to put in their savings accounts. This bounty was supposed to continue until they reached the age of twenty-one. Himmler also asked for annual reports on the health, weight and height of each of these favoured children.

Sometimes these gifts produced gratifying responses, such as this letter from Kathe Sayrl, a grateful mother from Mecklenburg:

> Thank you for your good wishes on the birth of my third Lebensborn child. The candlestick for little Helga has arrived safely, also the six bottles of Vitaborn juice. Please express my gratitude to the Reichsführer-SS from me and my husband. I enclose a picture taken at Christmas of three contented little girls – Giesela (October 1940), Dietlind (May 1942) and Helga (7 October 1943). Although it is difficult to bring up children in this, the fifth year of war, it is possible for every mother to do it with a proper attitude. For this, one needs a heart full of faith. It is quite clear to me that our leadership is doing everything to keep the young mothers happy and contented. But total war has only one response today – everything must be done for victory.

Her letter suggested that the propaganda being pumped out since the start of the war in favour of births, whether illegitimate or legitimate, had by now altered people's attitude to those women who had taken the exhortations literally:

> It is my particular pleasure to tell you that the desire to have a child is apparent in Mecklenburg, implanted even more firmly

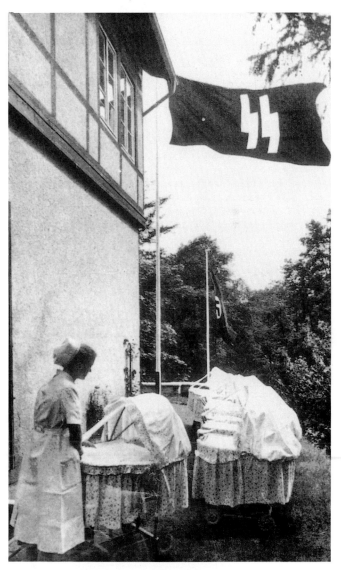

The stylised SS flag flies outside a Lebensborn home as "racially pure" babies are wheeled on to the terrace for fresh air.

(opposite, above)
A postcard
stresses the rural
character of the
homes.

(opposite, below)
Fresh air was
considered vital
to health, and the
children were
fully exposed to
it.

(above) The
ritualised SS
naming ceremony
for babies born at
Lebensborn homes,
where the baby is
named by an SS
officer and *(right)*
placed on a
cushion in front of
the swastika.

Das Heim Steinhöring in Bayern

Die Land-... vom ...gangstor ...steinhöring

Die Mütter-Häuser des „Lebensborns"

Phot.: Archiv Rasse- u. Siedlungshauptamt $$

Das Heim Klosterheide bei Lindow in der Mark

A poster is put up at a Polish village announcing an SS search.

An SS officer offers chocolate to a baby during a house-to-house search in Poland.

(*left*) Searching soldier peers through a window as mother and child prepare to be resettled by the Nazis.

(*below left*) Alexander Michelowski (left) in 1946, after he had been kidnapped by the Germans and liberated by the Allies.

(*below right*) Michelowski today.

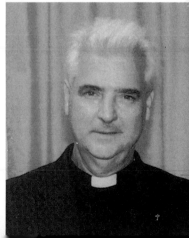

(*above*) Registration document for one of thousands of unknown and lost children, who is to be racially categorised and transported. On the reverse (*below*), beneath the SS Race Office stamp and date, is his racial assessment: N – d – ob (Nordic – dinarisch – ost baltic). This means he is a racial mix but with a good Nordic element, so he is acceptable.

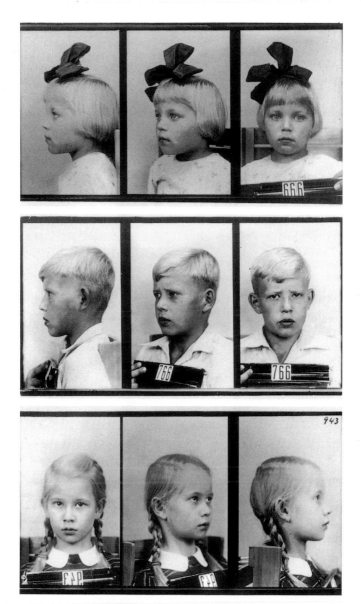

Children were numbered and photographed from three angles so that their racial characteristics could be analysed.

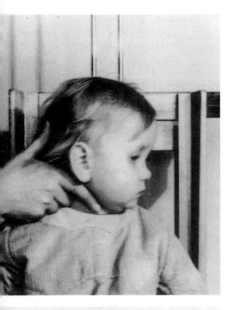

(*left and bottom left*) Even the youngest were racially tested and examined.

(*below*) Werner Thiermann, the son of a German soldier and a Norwegian woman and "adopted" by the Lebensborn organisation, seen at age three and (bottom) today.

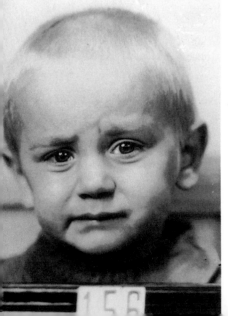

than it was. I can give you the example of my own experience. I had my first child at 18, when people said it was too early. When I had another one directly afterwards, people said I wouldn't be able to enjoy life. But now that I have had my third nobody says anything any more. Everyone realises what a marvellous thing I have done because in the course of this war people have come to understand that you can't offer anything more worthwhile than a whole brood of children.

Yet not everything was going as well in the Lebensborn homes as this letter might suggest. Himmler would occasionally make unannounced visits to them and was not always impressed with what he saw. In January 1941 he went to the Kurmark home at Klosterheide, near Berlin, and expressed his displeasure when he met Lebensborn officials a few days later. He was particularly worried about the popular image of the homes as breeding stations and even brothels – a reputation encouraged by the secrecy with which they were surrounded. He therefore decreed that male visitors should henceforth be restricted: 'The homes risk losing their good reputation through such visits. To avoid hardship a visitors' hut will be established in which visitors could be given coffee but where there will be no opportunity for intimacy.'

The suspicion was widespread that the Lebensborn homes not only provided facilities for expectant mothers but could also arrange liaisons between suitable potential mothers and fathers. Some thought that trysting places were provided in the homes themselves: among the documents presented at the Nuremberg trial was a letter to Himmler from a woman in Lübeck asking for information on the SS 'mating homes', because she wanted to make her contribution. His answer is not recorded.

What appears on the face of it to be firm evidence for the Lebensborn-as-stud-farm theory comes in the memoirs of an SS officer, Peter Neumann, published in Britain as *Other Men's Graves* (Weidenfeld & Nicolson, 1958). The book, translated from the French, is written in diary form and in a racy, dramatic style that suggests it is not totally free from invention. Yet much of Neumann's description of the fighting on the eastern front has the ring of authenticity, so his Lebensborn anecdote is worth relating. He tells of being summoned to see the Chief Medical Officer of the

SS, who informs him that research has been carried out into his racial history:

> I congratulate you. You are of pure Aryan stock. We've gone back as far as the 18th century and we've found nothing but completely Germanic stock in your ancestry.

Then Neumann is given a run-down of the genetic theory that individual characteristics are handed down from generation to generation ('Bach was one of a long line of musicians ... the Krupp dynasty has always given Germany inventors and technicians of genius'). There follows an argument in favour of stud farms for humans:

> It is quite normal to encourage the production of a perfect specimen among animals ... but people hold their hands up in horror at the idea of applying the same principle to the human species.

Neumann begins to get the drift. As he has only recently taken the SS oath of 'obedience unto death' he can hardly turn down this demanding assignment, and as he is a healthy young man of twenty he is anyway not inclined to. Two days later he and four other perfect Aryans are on the train to Marburg, where a car meets them for a two-hour drive to Schmallenog, in the Rothaar mountains. There they are taken to a modern building that looks like a hospital; whatever this institution may have been, it was not one of the recorded Lebensborn homes.

After another medical examination, which includes giving a semen specimen, Neumann is let loose among the women, almost immediately homing in on a small, perfectly formed blonde named Liselotte, who tells him she is a member of the BDM, the ultra-patriotic League of German Girls, and describes the moral pressure exerted on her to volunteer for this selfless duty. They talk about the morality of the transaction ('You aren't selling your body – you're giving it to Germany which is a very different matter') and then, after going to get their cards stamped to make it official, they spend six days and nights together before he goes back to his unit. From a passing reference in his diary nearly two years later, we learn that Liselotte presented the Führer with a son.

Another rumour suggested that there were SS-run apartments where the coupling could occur. Marc Hillel and Clarissa Henry noted in *Children of the SS* that, in the Steinhöring birth registers, numerous mothers gave one of four Munich apartments as their home address, and they wondered whether these served as impregnation centres. They appear, however, to have been the homes of officials at Lebensborn head office, and the addresses were probably supplied to mothers to enter on their documents when they wanted to preserve a measure of anonymity.

Surviving correspondence from Ebner suggests that he did not believe that finding partners for willing and lusty men and women was one of the functions of Lebensborn, and he often refused in blunt terms to fulfil the function of a dating agency. The most suggestive evidence that occasionally matches *were* made comes from Felix Kersten's memoirs. He claimed to recollect a conversation with his employer in 1943 which would seem to conflict with the Klosterheide memorandum two years earlier. According to Kersten, Himmler told him:

> I have made it known privately that any unmarried woman who is alone and longs for a child can turn to Lebensborn with perfect confidence. I would sponsor the child and provide for its education. I know this is a revolutionary step, because according to the existing middle-class code an unmarried woman has no right to yearn for a child ... Yet often she cannot find the right man or cannot marry because of her work, though her wish for a child is compelling. I have therefore created the possibility for such women to have the child they crave. As you can imagine, we recommend only racially faultless men as 'conception assistants'.

The Lebensborn homes were generally unpopular with ordinary Germans – especially, ironically enough, in the Nazi heartland of Bavaria. There were two main reasons for this. Naturally, the locals resented this highly privileged enclave in their midst, being given the best of scarce provisions. Worse, they knew that most of the mothers were unmarried and that many were planning to give their children up for adoption. That was what disturbed them most. Bavaria is a conservative, largely Catholic area where even today traditional moral standards and attitudes have survived longer than elsewhere. Even the most committed party member found it hard to swallow this apparent official condoning – even encouragement – of the conception of children out of wedlock.

In Steinhöring, fifty years on, it is hard to unravel what the villagers know now from what they knew then. It seems likely that the precise purpose of the home was never made clear to them officially, although they knew for certain that there was supposed to be something special about the babies born there. The secrecy surrounding it, and others like it across Germany and its satellites, gave rise to the darker rumours about what went on there. Throughout the nine-year history of the Lebensborn movement Himmler and his aides were forced to wage a constant battle to convince people that their ultimate aim of racial purity was so important as to override conventional moral considerations.

Although the whole concept of selective racial breeding is disgusting, the suggestion of random and wholesale loveless coupling is not wholly appropriate. While some of the pregnancies may well have been motivated by a woman's strong sense of duty to the state, or in some cases have been brought about by coercion, the scant available evidence suggests genuine affection between many of the mothers and their SS lovers. They were, after all, healthy young women with normal emotional needs.

One to whom we have spoken still keeps photographs of her daughter's father and his fond love-letters – bizarre mixtures of tenderness and patriotic exhortation – more than fifty years after he was executed by the Allies for crimes against humanity. And when, in 1985, the oldest part of the former home was demolished, some touching mementoes were found beneath the floorboards. They included signed photographs of handsome young men in SS uniform. 'From Max Wechter,' one reads, 'with happy memories.' And on another a young woman had written this simple inscription: 'My Captain'.

Yet the local prejudice against the homes was never eliminated. Even after so much time has passed, those who lived at Steinhöring throughout the war are still reluctant to discuss it. 'It was a blemish on our community,' von Feury recalled nearly fifty years later. 'In my opinion this SS racial breeding was one of the worst crimes of the Nazis. That is why people here no longer speak about it and don't want to know about it.' In part this is due to a lingering sense of national guilt and in part to the fear that their neighbours would disapprove of any breach of the unwritten but well-understood code of reticence.

One local woman, who worked as a nurse at the home just after the Americans liberated it, has been trying to build up a research archive about it, because of its significance in Germany's history; but she finds resistance to her enquiries from people who lived in the village during the war. Inevitably, there are those who, fifty years ago, held views and took actions of which today they are ashamed. There has therefore been a collective if unspoken decision to lock away the past and hide the key.

The Nazis' exhortations to the people to go forth and multiply had an effect in the years leading up to the war. By 1939 the birthrate was up to a peak of 20.4 live births per thousand population but three years later the figure was down to 14.9 – only fractionally higher than in 1933. So they were effectively back where they started. Nor did the campaign against abortions produce the desired results: the number rose steadily between 1940 and 1943 – the year the death penalty for abortion was introduced – and so did the number of miscarriages, many of them self-induced.

Worse still, the men of the SS let their *Reichsführer* down, at least as far as paternity was concerned, on a scale he must have found deeply disappointing. Far from the recommended average of four children per man, by 1939 they had reached only a paltry 1.1 – and even if you exclude the unmarried ones the figure was no more than 1.5. Although some childless SS families agreed to adopt children from the Lebensborn homes, most of them did not, preferring to be fined or even to leave the corps altogether.

Yet despite the stubborn refusal of the racial élite to make their required sacrifices at the altar of fertility, and despite the undercurrent of disapproval that the Lebensborn homes provoked in more traditional sections of German society, there was pressure on beds in them almost from the outset. As early as January 1940 Ebner wrote to Pflaum, then still in charge, saying th- the need for extra space was urgent. New homes filled up almost as soon as they were opened.

Room also had to be found later on for young children from

occupied countries who, after careful racial screening to ensure an ample supply of good Aryan genes, were to be 'Germanised' and sent to Lebensborn homes to be readied for adoption. At the beginning the organisation had been responsible only for placing those born in its own homes, but now it had to gear up to handle children whose pedigree was uncertain – like a motor manufacturer's showroom, set up to sell new cars of its own make, now obliged to distribute second-hand models from other factories. Although Lebensborn homes were instituted in nearly all the occupied countries, many of these foreign-born children were sent to Germany.

Space was not the only problem in the war years: staffing the homes was a constant headache too. On the medical side, each home was under the control of an SS doctor, backed up by an administrative head, a secretary and a senior sister – usually one of the ideologically sound 'Brown Sisters' of the NSV. There was a nurse for the mothers and another for the children, as well as security guards, maintenance staff and domestic workers. A pediatrician from a nearby town would normally be on call if needed, seeing each child every four weeks and passing on instructions to the nurses. Every month clinical reports were sent to the Lebensborn gynaecologist based at the Munich headquarters, and a nutritionist was also available there to advise on the mothers' diet. When Himmler became concerned about infant mortality, the professional back-up was increased.

As soon as war broke out, doctors were badly needed to treat the wounded in field hospitals, and had it not been for Himmler's personal involvement it would have been virtually impossible to keep them within the organisation. Yet in spite of his chief's interventions, Ebner's staffing problems multiplied. Some doctors frankly disapproved of the purpose of the homes and treated the women with overt disrespect.

Even the Brown Sisters did not always come up to Ebner's high standard. In a memo in 1940, he complained that they did not stay at the homes long enough but kept leaving at their own request. Some were inadequately trained in the care of expectant and nursing mothers. Most serious, in his view, was their attitude to unmarried mothers, many looking down on them, as the doctors did. (This sprang from the ideology of the sisterhood, which insisted that they must leave the service if they became pregnant out of wedlock themselves.) All the same, Ebner preferred them to the 'Blue Sisters' or nuns, whose primary loyalty was to the Church rather than to the party. To ease the nursing problem, Ebner agreed that suitable mothers, after rudimentary training, could stay on at the homes to care for others; at least he could be fairly confident of their positive attitude. He also arranged with the Health Ministry that, for trainee nurses, a year at a Lebensborn home could count as a qualification equal to a probationary year at a children's hospital.

Yet some mothers were so upset by the attitude of doctors and nurses towards them that they refused offers to stay on as nurses, even when they had no other job to go to. In 1942 Lydia Ossig, who had a baby at the Wienerwald home, wrote to Himmler complaining about Sister Gerda, apparently a classic battleaxe. Lydia had been dancing with a friend in the day room when Gerda came in to admonish them. 'You should be ashamed dancing like this at this time,' they were told. 'You know the doctor has forbidden it.' This provoked Lydia to denounce Gerda to the *Reichsführer* for her 'dreadful attitude'. She explained: 'She is two-faced and talks about one mother in front of the others.'

While in complaining mode, Lydia went on to express her resentment at privileges given to one particular mother because the father of her child was a high SS official. 'She has a double room to herself, even though the home is full, and she is allowed to go in and see her baby, which the rest aren't.' Lydia concluded the letter with an apology for bothering Himmler with the matter, but 'I can't possibly consider working in a place that employs someone like Sister Gerda'.

By a coincidence, among Lebensborn documents to have survived is a long report on Sister Gerda made before she was accepted into the organisation. It goes into intricate detail about her racial background, 'Nordic with Dinaric influences', and assesses her attitude, which is found to 'fit in with SS principles'. She is additionally lauded as 'inwardly a strong Nazi'. Lydia might well have agreed with all that, although not with the further observation that the sister was 'friendly to the mothers'.

It is unlikely that Himmler had much sympathy for Lydia's complaint, for he himself insisted on strict standards of behaviour in the organisation and Sister Gerda may only have been obeying his orders. This letter from Ebner to Sollmann illustrates the point:

Dear Sollmann,

As you know, the Reichsführer-SS is a strong opponent of excessive beauty care in our women. He considers it unworthy of the German woman to paint her lips, pluck her eyebrows and paint her nails. We hold to this very strongly in the Lebensborn homes, and ensure that the mothers do not start these unfortunate habits. Unfortunately I have noticed that women working at head office do indulge in these deplorable practices. Some of the mothers have noticed it and are somewhat confused about what the real attitude of the SS is in this respect. It would therefore be better if the women who work for Lebensborn set a proper example.

Lebensborn homes were set up in other countries in the wake of the German advances in the early days of the war. Partly these were to take care of the children of local mothers, fathered by German soldiers and SS men. If the mother was of racially sound stock, these children would make good Germans. The homes also had a role in the Germanisation of suitable children of local parents. There were three Lebensborn homes in Poland, two in Austria, one each in Belgium, Holland, France, Luxembourg and Denmark. In Norway, where the blonde local women were thought to mate exceptionally well with Germans, no fewer than nine homes were established, not strictly speaking part of the Lebensborn organisation but closely allied to it. Some 6,000 children, fathered by Germans, were born in them to Norwegian mothers. The total of all Norwegian children with German wartime fathers could be as much as ten times that.

At his Nuremberg trial Max Sollmann estimated that 12,000 children were born in Lebensborn homes, excluding Norway, in the nine years of their existence, but this is probably an exaggeration. The records are incomplete but they show that between 1936 and September 1943 the total of births was 5,047. To reach Sollmann's figure, another 7,000 would have had to be born in the remaining twenty months until the end of the war – and since the homes were being progressively closed as the Allies overran them, this seems highly improbable. If the 1936–43 figure is correct, it would be surprising if more than 7,500 children were born in the homes altogether.

The number of unmarried women admitted to them increased from year to year initially, and they were nearly always in a majority. Until

1939, according to Ebner, 57.6 per cent of the mothers were single, rising to around 70 per cent by 1942. Only towards the end of the war did the homes cater to a majority of married women, many of them the wives of Nazi officials and SS men seeking to have their children as far away as they could from the advancing enemy and from the cities, by then under the constant threat of Allied bombing.

After years of a patriotic war fuelled by repeated expressions of Messianic certainty about the inevitability of victory and the rightness of the cause, the possibility of defeat takes time to absorb. Through most of 1944 the Lebensborn organisation went competently about its business of producing and distributing perfect racial specimens to populate the Thousand Year Reich. Himmler continued to make speeches articulating his Utopian vision and continued to pen little homilies on the domestic arrangements. It was only towards the end of the year that the real significance of the Allies' Normandy landings in June and the disastrous reverses on the eastern front began to sink in. In 1944, the autumn leaves that fell in the woods surrounding Himmler's fountains of life signalled the approach of something more terminal than winter.

5

Himmler's Children

> In the SS I have systematically defied existing laws and explained to my men that children are always a great blessing, legitimate or not. What's been the result? Now my men tell me with shining eyes that they have just had an illegitimate child. The girls regard it as an honour, not a disgrace.
>
> *Himmler to Felix Kersten, May 1943*

As the twentieth century closes, the super-children born of racially impeccable parents in the Lebensborn homes are in their fifties. There must be thousands of them in Germany, many with their own children and grandchildren, yet it is exceedingly hard to track them down.

The reason is plain. They were infants at the end of the war, that cathartic time when all the attitudes and certainties of the society they were born to were suddenly turned on their head. For a mother, it had been a matter of pride to be bearing the child of an SS man, custom-bred as a specimen of the projected new racial élite; now suddenly it became a matter for shame. The women's role in the transaction no longer had the heroic overtones that Himmler had vested in it. Instead, it was regarded as a biological aberration, a gruesome attempt to give effect to theoretical principles that were now seen as calculating, manipulative and more than a little deranged.

Small wonder, then, that the mothers were inhibited about revealing the facts to their children or to anyone else. Many of the children had been adopted and their new parents would equally have seen no purpose in telling them the truth about their origins; indeed, they would have believed, with some justification, that being frank and open could cause more psychological harm than good.

That is why, when we did come across Lebensborn children and mothers, they asked for anonymity. In the story that follows the names have been invented but the facts are true.

Inge is over eighty now. Her daughter Greta was born in 1944 at the Lebensborn home at Steinhöring, the fruit of a passionate affair with a married SS officer, some years older than Inge, who was executed by the Allies for war crimes in 1946. We spoke to both women at Inge's home, where she and Greta were leafing through some photographs taken at Steinhöring soon after Greta was born. There was an album full of them. The very fact that so many pictures were taken – of children, doctors, nurses and other staff – is a clue to the affection in which the mothers held the Lebensborn homes and to the spirit of community that was fostered in the best of them, as at a well-motivated school or college.

There was then no sense of guilt, despite the disapproval of traditionalists outside. The women were honoured to be part of the Nazi system, doing what they had been persuaded was their duty to the Fatherland. Some in any case were married and those who were not, such as Inge, had a genuine reason to be relieved at the more liberal attitude to illegitimacy manifested in the homes. They viewed them as an enlightened social service.

'This was your first smile,' said Inge, as she came across a fuzzy photo of a baby laid out on a blanket. 'Look at the funny leggings you're wearing. At two months you were very lively for your age, and very inquisitive; but in this other one you are still a bit serious.'

Greta turned to another picture. 'This must be the nursing sister. She looks very friendly.'

'Yes, she was. She smiled at me a lot. They were all very nice. I used to send them films for their cameras – they weren't easy to get hold of – and they would take pictures of you and send them back to me, with letters telling me how you were getting on. One of the sisters was so fond of you that she even used to take you out in the pram when she went shopping. She said she liked your flashing blue eyes.

'Look, here's one taken when you were teething. You were always very weepy then. And this is one when you were eight months old, in June. I'd left the home then but I came to visit you and stayed for a fortnight. I used to go whenever I could get time off from work, but it wasn't easy because there were no direct trains and the service was often interrupted by air-raid warnings. I was always very sad to have to go back home again.

'See those shoes? The sister had got them for you. I think she must have taken them from one of the other children. They look good on you.'

Inge stayed at the home for four weeks after Greta's birth. She had mixed feelings about leaving: on the one hand she found the petty restrictions at the home irksome, but she felt desolate about having to abandon her only child. Still, she had a job to go back to and she needed to support herself. Even if it were feasible to set up house with her daughter, there was no doubt that the baby would be better looked-after at Steinhöring, because it was well known that the Lebensborn homes received special allowances of foods that were scarce in wartime – meat, fruit and dairy produce. So it was not too difficult for Inge to suppress her feelings of guilt and self-reproach.

'I always looked forward to coming to visit you in the holidays,' she told Greta as they looked through the photographs together. 'But it was also sad for me, because I knew I would have to go away again. That was terrible, although I knew you were very well taken care of. And you couldn't have stayed with me because where I lived they didn't allow children.'

The sisters at the home would write with regular progress reports on the baby, and Inge has kept their letters, meticulously detailed and overflowing with good news. Greta began to read from some of them: 'She starts to flirt as soon as I get near her playpen . . . she is especially interested in my spectacles and reaches up to touch them whenever she can . . . her hair has already become quite thick and curly . . . she is a saucy little thing, a little ray of pure sunshine . . . already, she perks up when you call her name.'

Several of the pictures showed the Steinhöring home, and Greta, who had recently visited it with us, told her mother how things had changed in the twenty years or so since they last paid a visit there together. The outbuildings, which mostly housed the staff and guards, are gone today and the garden has been enlarged for the benefit of the severely handicapped people who now live there. There were pictures of the lake, virtually unchanged, and some of the trees were also recognisable.

'You really were a very sweet thing,' said Inge on seeing one of the photographs, 'I have to admit that.' Coming to another picture, she looked up quickly and stared hard at Greta. 'You looked like your father. Exactly like him; to a T. The smile, the snub nose, the hands, the posture. He even had dimples like that.'

Until that point it could have been any other elderly mother being visited by her daughter and looking nostalgically through the family album. Suddenly, though, there was real tension in the air. The two women had very different perceptions of Greta's father. To Inge, he was the handsome hero, the love of her life. Greta, of course, had no first-hand recollection of him. To her, as to most of her generation, the SS were a fanatical group whose madness had caused millions of deaths in Europe. This was not an uncommon dichotomy in postwar Germany; but the special circumstances of Greta's birth threw it into sharper relief.

Inge and Gunter had met on holiday. 'It was a real love story,' Inge insists. 'A great love.' When she discovered she was pregnant Gunter was delighted and, because of his position in the SS, he was easily able to arrange for her to be cared for in a Lebensborn home.

Inge had mixed feelings about the forthcoming birth. At first she was shocked. 'Naturally I wanted a child but when it actually happens one suddenly feels one's moral courage draining away. But in spite of that I looked forward to it.' At least she knew that at the Lebensborn home she could have her child in peace, security and – just as important – secrecy. That was a vital consideration in the climate of the time.

Both parents had wanted a son so that he could grow up to be like Gunter. When Greta failed them in this respect, Inge quickly found consolation in that she looked so much like her father. It is hard to tell at this distance in time whether the likeness is merely a product of Inge's wishful thinking; but she insists that Greta speaks very much as Gunter did and, like him, has a quick and passionate temper. 'It was a great happiness for me that she was so obviously his daughter. His family were very kind. His two sisters were very good to Greta while Gunter was away fighting.'

Greta's feelings, now that she is a middle-aged woman and knows all about her father, are very different. The truth about her birth was revealed to her only gradually. At fifteen she was told she was illegitimate. Not until she was over forty did she learn that Gunter had been executed as a war criminal.

She had effectively forced her mother to confess about the circumstances of her birth on a summer's day in 1957 when they were walking in the woods near their home. For months – years, even – she had been trying to pluck up the courage to ask. She had been aware of some undefined mystery surrounding her almost since 1946, when her mother and grandmother had gone to collect her from the home and taken her on the long, uncomfortable train journey to the city. That journey is among her first vivid memories: she can recall the ruins of the bombed-out stations on the route and her terror that the two women were going to abandon her in one of them.

The two women and the child lived in a small two-roomed apartment. At first there was nothing unusual about there being no man in the house: thousands of German soldiers who had survived the war were still being held prisoner by the Allies. Between 1946 and 1949 most of them came back. Greta's family's apartment was on a main road and she remembers seeing scores of released prisoners walk along it towards their wives' houses. Some stopped to ask the way and people gave them bread. Children in her class at school would suddenly say one morning: 'My father has come back.'

Greta was never told specifically that her own father would never make that heart-stopping journey to their front door, because Inge thought she was not old enough to cope with the realisation. For years, therefore, Greta would dream about his arrival: she was convinced in her mind that he would come in the afternoon. The apartment was on the third floor and, for a while, every time the doorbell rang her heart pounded and she went to the top of the stairs to look down, hoping against hope that it would be him. As the years went by and the joyous moment did not come, she gradually came to accept that she would never see him. When other children walked in the street with their fathers, she would feel a pang of envy and longing.

As she grew older she became more curious about her father. She found it hard to quiz her mother, who was never easy to confide in – probably because they had lived apart for the first four years of her life. Finally she steeled herself to put a question about something that troubled her greatly: how was it that she was called by Inge's maiden name? All the other children she knew, even those whose father was dead, had taken his surname. Inge explained, not too convincingly, that by chance both she and Gunter shared the same surname before their marriage. Greta found that hard to believe and for a while, searching her mind frantically for explanations, she wondered whether Inge was really her mother at all.

All she had been told about Gunter was that he was a strong, warm-hearted and fair man and that Inge loved him very much. But over time she noticed that her relatives and other acquaintances would react oddly when his name came into the conversation. For years she was taken every Sunday to see her mother's brother and his family, and she noticed something strange about the way they all spoke to her, always with a hint of condescension. She later learned that her uncle had been a strong Nazi supporter during the war but like many Germans had been quick to denounce Hitler after the surrender. After she discovered the truth about her father, she reasoned that her uncle and others were somehow resolving the contradiction in their attitude to the Nazis by taking it out on her, a living reminder of the Hitler years.

She began to have the feeling that she was being treated as something of a sideshow in front of other adults. One Sunday, when she was at her uncle's house as usual, the family had visitors. The grown-ups sat talking in the living room while she played outside. Her cousin was sent out with a message that she should go and join the adults. Greta sensed that they had been talking about her and, embarrassed, refused to obey the summons. Her cousin tried to push her through the door but she hurled herself to the ground and refused to budge. In the end she had to be dragged in, whereupon her cousin announced to the visitors: 'That's her.' Presumably the visitors had heard of Gunter and were curious to see his daughter. The same sort of thing happened once or twice more on visits to other relatives, though not quite so brutally. For the most part people were polite and tried to be kind, but Greta sensed a lack of spontaneity.

Growing up in Germany in the 1940s and 1950s, it was inevitable that she should hear about the Nazis and the things they had done during their years of power. There was some talk about it among her friends at school – although remarkably little was taught about it in class – and Greta wanted to discuss it with her mother. Inge, though, was reticent. When Greta brought up the subject, she quickly steered the conversation to another topic. At fifteen, Greta decided it was time for her questions to be answered. The walk in the woods was the opportunity she had been seeking.

'It is time you told me the truth about my birth,' she said. Her mother stopped walking and looked hard at the young girl fast approaching maturity, again reflecting on how like Gunter she looked.

'Your father was a good man,' she said, repeating a formula she had used a hundred times before. She sensed that this bland answer would not satisfy Greta in her present mood but at least it gave Inge time to collect her thoughts.

'You know I don't mean that. I want to know how you met him, when you were married, how he died in the war, who he *really* was.'

Inge had known this time would come. She had never been planning to keep the truth – or at least not all of it – from Greta for ever. She sensed that, if she did not respond to her daughter's urgent probing now, there was a danger of alienating her for good.

The walk turned into a confession. Inge admitted to Greta not only that she had never been married but that Gunter had been married to someone else and had several other children. Looking back, Greta believes that it was this, the fact that she had half-brothers and sisters she had never seen or even been told about, that grieved and offended her most. The walk ended in silence. When they returned home she went to her room to collect her thoughts.

She knew her mother had kept a bundle of letters that Gunter had written her. When she came downstairs she asked if she might be allowed to read them. At first Inge refused.

'These are personal letters,' she protested. 'They were not written to be read by anyone except me – not even by you. They contain many personal things.'

Greta persisted. 'I have the right to read them. He is my father and he is dead and these letters are all he has left behind. It is the only chance I will ever have to get to know him.'

Inge gave in and brought the letters down from her room. Greta sat reading for the rest of the evening. They were good letters – loving, solicitous and with a touch of humour. They were unfailingly optimistic about the progress of the war. Gunter assured Inge that all would be well when victory was achieved and they could see each other again. He always made solicitous enquiries about the baby's health and said that if there was anything they needed he would try, as an influential SS officer, to obtain it for them.

On first reading the letters, Greta's reaction was one of elation. Here was a man she thought she would have liked. Over the next days and weeks she read the letters over and over again for clues about him and his relationship with her mother. Few love-letters improve from such sustained scrutiny and soon she recognised that they were packed with romantic clichés, as well as false optimism. ('It is very hard here at the front,' he would write, 'but morale is good and courage is of a high order.')

Now that one of the curtains separating her from her past had been raised, Greta was hungry for more information. But she had to proceed with caution. Inge had always felt a lingering sense of guilt about abandoning her child during her formative years, even though in the circumstances of the time it was hard to see what alternative she had: certainly she could not have matched the quality of physical care or diet that was available at Steinhöring. Greta sensed this feeling and had to be careful that she did not seem to be reproaching her mother in any way, or to be doubting the truth of what she told her. If any suggestion of that filtered into her questions, Inge would clam up. As a result, key questions about her mother's true motives and feelings – questions to which Greta would dearly have loved an answer – remained unasked.

Her mother's revelations increased the sense of isolation and rejection that had been instilled in Greta by other people's often unconsciously wary treatment of her. She has never married and believes that this is an important part of the reason. 'I feel that I have never done anything but look at life through a glass wall that prevents me from participating in it fully,' she says in retrospect.

It was more than twenty-five years after that walk in the forest that Greta discovered the whole truth about her father's war record and about the true racial nature of the Lebensborn movement in which she was born. As she developed into a woman, she recognised that there were things her mother was keeping from her. Only when she was nearly forty did it seem imperative to uncover the entire story. She decided to do some independent research.

It was not easy. The staff at the Document Centre in Berlin, where the Nazi archives are kept, refused to give her access to them because she was not a qualified historian. But scores of war histories have been published and she spent hours in libraries going through their indexes. Eventually she found the reference she sought. With growing horror, she read details of the war crimes her father had committed and the number of deaths – of Jews, communists and gypsies – for which he was said to have been responsible.

She came out of the library numb, shattered and confused. Her first reaction was that she had to keep the information secret: her friends must never know, or they would shun her. Then, perversely, she began to feel that the only way she could begin to purge her inherited guilt was to rush on to the streets and shout the truth to the world. She remembered her mother telling her repeatedly how like her father she looked, how similar were many of her individual characteristics. What if the evil in him, too, had been transferred to her? She recalled times when she had lost her temper with colleagues and had behaved with irrational fury. Didn't that prove that the genes had been passed on?

In the event she neither shouted the news from the rooftops nor kept it completely to herself, but told a few of her most intimate friends. They did their best to comfort her. They pointed out that she was not herself a war criminal and could not be held accountable for her father's actions. Greta, though, found it hard to make the distinction. She felt that as Gunter's daughter she could not be absolved from some inherited responsibility for his evils.

There was another, perhaps even more terrible way in which she was inextricably involved. Her birth had been part of a programme aimed at producing a pure Aryan race. The deaths that her father had initiated were another aspect of the same programme, with the purpose of wiping out what the Nazis saw as defiling influences. There was a sense, therefore, in which Gunter may have regarded his children as replacement stock for those he was eliminating. She wondered bitterly for which particular Jew or gypsy she had been designated a substitute.

These dreadful thoughts were not to be assuaged by friends, however well-meaning, telling her that she could not be held account-able for the deeds of her father. She felt compelled to intensify her researches into his career, although the same friends tried to dissuade her, saying that it was fruitless to look back; that what had happened had happened. When, at her friends' persuasion, she sought psychological help the therapist, too, advised her to drop her enquiries; but she could not. She persevered and eventually gained access to the official documents. She pressed on partly because the subject was beginning to obsess her and partly because she told herself – although in truth with little conviction – that if she dug deep enough she might find extenuating circumstances, or at least an account of some individual act of mercy that would have confirmed her father's humanity.

After a while she realised that this approach was fruitless. The reality was inescapable. His crimes were certainly not unique, but they were crimes and he had been properly punished for them. Exculpation was no answer, nor would it help to turn a blind eye. An important stage in coming to terms with the enormity of his actions was when she was able to say to herself and to her friends: 'Yes, my father was a murderer – but I am another person.' In effect she found herself in the position of Germany itself. Though recognising how important it is to acknowledge and expose the crimes of the Nazis and to draw lessons from the past, the Germans of the 1990s do not see how they can be expected to make amends in perpetuity, any more than Greta should spend the rest of her life seeking absolution for her father's sins. She would never stop being ashamed of him, but he no longer obsessed her.

The present use of the Highland Home is a massive irony. It remained a children's hospital until 1971, when it was turned into a home for severely disabled adults. Patients displaying grave physical and mental handicaps are now cared for in the very rooms where, fifty years ago, a race was being raised as a central part of a project to eliminate such imperfect specimens from the face of the Thousand Year Reich. Any child then who, despite its impeccable breeding, showed symptoms to compare with those of today's residents would have been a candidate for euthanasia.

Forty-five years after her mother took her home from Steinhöring, Greta went back. It was not her first return visit. Like many other Lebensborn children, she had made the pilgrimage to her birthplace not long after being told of her origins. She had taken her mother with her and met a women who had been a nurse at the home and whom her mother thought she recognised from a photograph – but, like all the other nurses in the same position, she claimed that she had not gone to work there until mid-1945, after the SS had left. Greta, who had also studied the photograph, was convinced that she was one of the nurses who had looked after her, and was disappointed by her persistent denial.

Much had changed since the war, but the iron gate still carried the SS sign and its original runic symbols, so beloved of Himmler. The swastikas had been removed but the other signs were allowed to stay, presumably because nobody would notice them unless they were searching for them specifically.

The statue of a mother breast-feeding her child was still there, partly concealed among shrubs. While Greta deplored its awful associations, she could recognise it as a powerful and in some ways a beautiful work of art. The sunlight filtered through the leaves to make a pattern of white specks, like stars, on the stone.

The old building, the former priests' home, had been pulled down but the new wing, built for Himmler in the 1930s, is still there, although the layout has changed. The large dining hall has been broken up into smaller spaces to accommodate the mentally handicapped people who are now in occupation. The upstairs hall has similarly disappeared. That was the venue for the bizarre naming ritual which Greta, along with every other child born there, had been made to endure.

Although she was so small when she left, Greta believed she could just recall the upstairs room that she shared with three other children. And she thought she dimly remembered other occurrences, such as the times she had cried and nobody had come to her.

After looking round the house she walked across the park at the back, past the ornamental lake – unchanged since the war – to the buildings of the old railway station, now mostly used for storing grain. That was where, until almost the very last days before the surrender, trains would arrive laden with food and other supplies for the homes, thanks to Himmler's personal insistence that the mothers and their children should never go short.

Returning across the lawn to the back of the home, Greta observed: 'I wonder what kind of things happened to me here, what it was really like for me. These were the steps that I've seen in the photographs with the prams standing on the terrace in line. I think I can remember scrambling up them once, but I suppose I might have invented that.

'I know I am a part of the history of this place yet I do not feel at all connected to it. It is like something I have read about in a book. I have come to terms with the circumstances of my birth. To be truthful, it all leaves me quite cold.'

6

Poles Like Us

Obviously in such a mixture of peoples there will always be some
racially good types. Therefore I think that it is our duty to take
their children with us, to remove them from their environment, if
necessary by robbing or stealing them.

Himmler, October 1943

Lying between Germany and Russia, with choice slices of its territory
coveted by each, Poland has always been a victim of other countries'
quarrels and ambitions. Hitler's occupation of the Polish port of
Danzig (Gdansk) in September 1939, allied to his transparent intention of bringing Poland into his planned eastern empire, signalled
the start of the Second World War, in which six million Poles – a
sixth of the population – would be killed, including virtually all the
country's three million Jews. Most were killed by the Germans but
some by the Russians, who occupied the eastern part of Poland at
the beginning of the war.

When the war started the western part of the country, closest to
the German border and inhabited chiefly by ethnic Germans, was
incorporated into the German Reich. The rest of the country, where
the inferior races lived, was given a separate Nazi administration and
dubbed the 'General Government'. In October 1939 Himmler was
appointed as 'Commissar for Consolidating German Nationhood',
with the responsibility for ensuring that Germany's racial policies
were extended to Poland and other occupied territories. Primarily
this meant seeking the Final Solution of the Jewish question, but
his duties also included identifying ethnic Germans and others
whose racial stock was pure enough for them to be accepted as
Germans.

'My aim has always been the same,' he declared in 1940, 'to attract all the Nordic blood in the world and take it for ourselves.'

The Nazis' plans for Poland were clear and specific and not limited to military conquest. The aim was to obliterate the nation entirely. Ethnic Germans, as long as they were willing to consider themselves as Germans rather than Poles, would be settled in the western regions in the former homes of non-German Poles, who were to be moved to the General Government territory, where they would be treated as slaves. Other Poles, if they matched up to the strict racial criteria, would be allowed to opt, if they wished, for 'Germanisation', which would mean giving up all traces of their native culture and language. This privilege would not be extended to people with a record of leftist political activity.

In 1939, after the success of the military campaign in Poland, RuSHA issued a paper entitled 'The treatment of the population in former Polish areas according to racial-political criteria'. It suggested confiscating Polish property and farmland. Like the Jews in Germany, Poles in Poland would be barred from many trades, crafts and professions. Church services in Polish were to be banned and specifically Polish holy days abolished. Polish clubs, associations, restaurants, cinemas and theatres were to be closed down and the possession of radio sets and gramophones prohibited.

The most far-reaching part of the programme laid down that Polish children could not be educated except on strictly German terms. Only a rudimentary form of education would be offered in Poland itself, at *Volksschulen* where children were merely taught to count to five hundred, to write their names and to obey the Germans without question. Higher education would be restricted to Germany and would be available only to the children of those Poles who agreed to, and were accepted for, Germanisation.

The one flaw in the scheme was that it could deprive the new German Reich of a potentially valuable resource in the children of Poles who had demonstrably good racial credentials although they might not necessarily be recognised as ethnic Germans – or might be stubbornly unwilling to regard themselves as anything but Polish. If caught young enough, some of these children could be Germanised to increase the national stock of Aryan blood. When Himmler and his generals toured Poland at the beginning of the occupation, they were surprised by the number of blond, fair-skinned children, with just the attributes they saw as the most desirable. It was, they knew, fruitless to try to make diehard Polish adults into good Germans, whatever their skin complexion. Young children, though, were different, as Himmler recognised.

'In the course of the next ten years,' he said soon after the invasion, 'the population of the General Government will become a permanently inferior race, which will be available to us for slave labour. A fundamental question is the racial screening and sifting of the young. It is obvious that in this mixture of people some very good racial types will appear from time to time.'

Provided these children passed a thorough physical examination they could, after intensive brainwashing, be made to forget that they were ever Poles at all. A prerequisite of this was that all links with their Polish parents must be comprehensively severed and the children's names changed. This would not only strengthen Germany but would have the additional benefit of weakening the Polish blood-line.

The RuSHA paper laid down:

There must be an attempt to exclude racially valuable children from the resettlement [of Poles] and to educate them in suitable institutions, such as the former military orphanages in Potsdam, or in a German family. To be suitable, children must not be more than eight or ten years old, because as a rule a genuine ethnic transformation – that is, a final Germanisation – is possible only up to this age. The first condition for this is a complete ban on all links with their Polish relatives. The children will be given German names of Teutonic origin. Their birth and heredity certificates will be kept by a special department.

Himmler entertained no doubts about the prospects for the success of the project. In a memorandum dated May 1940 he wrote:

We have faith above all in this our own blood, which has flowed into a foreign nationality through the vicissitudes of German history. We are convinced that our own philosophy and ideals will reverberate in the spirit of these children who resemble us racially.

For a time he had to fend off attempts by the NVS, the state adoption agency, to take over the scheme for itself, but Hitler was on Himmler's side and there was never any real doubt that the SS, via Lebensborn, would be given the responsibility. In June 1940 Himmler wrote to Arthur Greiser, Gauleiter of the Danzig (Gdansk) region, spelling out his plans in detail. Polish children of proper breeding would be identified and taken into the care of the Lebensborn organisation, on the pretext that their health was at risk in the families or orphanages where they lived. If their racial credentials checked out they should be subjected to a period of intense Germanisation and given to good German families. And he had a ready answer to those who questioned the morality of stealing children, as he explained in a much-quoted speech to his generals in October 1943:

They say: 'How can you be so cruel to take a child away from its mother?' To that I answer: 'How can *you* be so cruel, to leave a brilliant future enemy on the other side, who will kill your sons and your grandsons?'

A prime source of supply of these new Germans would be Polish orphanages, then filled with children whose parents had been removed or liquidated by the Germans. Himmler and his associates spread the word that many ethnically German children had been taken by the Poles into orphanages and their names changed to prevent their racial origin from being recognised. While this may have been true in some cases, it was used as a pretext to Germanise any likely-looking orphan and to follow in reverse the procedure the Poles were said to have employed. In February 1942 SS Colonel Ulrich Greifelt, a member of Himmler's staff who was later convicted of war crimes at Nuremberg, wrote a long directive on the procedure to be followed in dealing with the children:

There is a large number of children staying at former Polish orphanages or with Polish foster parents who must be regarded as children of Nordic descent on account of their outward appearance. Investigations have shown that all orphans who descended from ethnic German parents were in the past systematically taken by the Poles to Polish orphanages as foundlings, or given to Polish foster parents. They were given Polish names, and documents showing their true descent are not available.

This was a convenient notion to propagate, because it meant that any orphan whose appearance fitted the Germans' blueprint could be claimed as one of their own. Greifelt went on to say that, to be restored to the German nation, these children should be subjected to racial tests at Lodz, the Polish headquarters of the Race and Settlement Office, then go for six weeks of psychological appraisal and character analysis by Dr Hildegard Hetzer at the children's homes at Brockau and Kalisz.

One of the victims of the procedure was Helena Wilkanowicz, who was at the orphanage at Pabjanice, near Lodz, when SS inspectors went there in 1943. Nearly thirty years later she told Clarissa Henry and Marc Hillel:

Three SS men came into the room and put us up against a wall. There were about 100 children altogether. They immediately picked out the fair children with blue eyes – seven altogether, including me, though I do not have a drop of German blood in my veins. I was 12 years old at the time. My father, who tried to stop my being taken away, was threatened by the soldiers. They even said he would be taken to a concentration camp. But I have no idea what happened to him later because we were taken immediately to the children's reception camp at Brockau.

Maria Hanfova, one of the children taken at the Lidice massacre in Czechoslovakia in 1942 (an act of brutal German revenge for the assassination of the governor of Bohemia and Moravia), described her examination by Dr Hetzer:

We were made to undress completely, boys and girls alike. The lady measured our heads, chests and hips. Then we were weighed one after the other on some big scales in the corner. After that we had our face photographed from all angles. We were half dead with fear.

Thousands of pictures of the heads of children from the occupied countries, most of them taken from three angles, were discovered after the war at Kalisz, Lodz and elsewhere. They can be inspected today at the headquarters of the Commission to Investigate Nazi War Crimes in Warsaw. It is an affecting sight – row upon row of boxes stuffed with pictures of children, some no more than a year old, others up to twelve, meticulously numbered. Most look frightened, some are crying and all are obviously confused. No doubt many live in Germany today with new names and identities, perhaps unaware of their true origin; for only about 20 per cent returned to Poland after the war.

Of the children identified in the preliminary examinations and tests as being of potentially valuable racial stock, those between six and twelve would be sent to German boarding schools where, according to Greifelt's instructions, they would be treated in all respects like German children. Those between two and six went to Lebensborn homes, where they would be added to the stock of German children for adoption. Greifelt's directive laid down that their true national origin would not be revealed to prospective parents:

> Special care must be taken that the expression 'Polish children suitable for Germanisation' is not made public to the detriment of the children. The children are rather to be described as 'German orphans from the regained Eastern territories'.

This was a considerate precaution, for so fierce was the anti-Polish sentiment whipped up by Nazi propagandists that to describe some-body as a Pole was to invite ridicule and even worse. And it fitted in with the Nazis' belief that almost any horror could be countenanced if you thought up a sufficiently innocuous euphemism for it. There would be scant proof of the true nature of the crime, and less chance of a comeback. For people who could refer to the liquidation of the Jews as 'freeing the ghetto', 'relocation' and 'transporting eastwards', this little white lie about the Polish children was a small matter, quite routine.

Another significant directive, issued by the German Ministry of the Interior in December 1942, provides poignant evidence of the agony caused to the relatives of the selected children, who by now were being taken direct from their family homes as well as from orphanages. Referring to the Kalisz centre, then being used for the indoctrination programme, the directive stated:

It has been shown in the course of time that it must be expected that remaining Polish relatives and friends will attempt to find the location of the children. This could be done at any time by inquiring at the local police registration office. That, however, would endanger the children's Germanisation. Setbacks to their education, which may occur if the children come under the influence of their relatives, must be avoided at all costs. I therefore request that a separate police registration office be established for that home, to be known as Police/Registration Office II in Kalisz/Warthegau.

The request was granted.

Rogozno is a nondescript little town some forty kilometres north of Poznan in Wielkopolska, the heart of the original Polish nation. Just off the main road from Poznan to the Baltic, it serves as the centre of a farming community. Its short high street is lined with small shops and other buildings from the nineteenth century, dominated by a church with a characteristic onion dome. The grey railway station, with the date 1881 inscribed above the entrance, is about a kilometre from the town centre, down a road which today has houses built alongside it but which in 1943 went through open fields.

On a September morning in that year a curious procession made its way along the road from the town to the station. At its head was a group of some two dozen children, aged from twelve to as young as two, the youngest being looked after by nurses in white aprons. A few of the children were animated, laughing boisterously together, for they had been told they were going on holiday. Most, though, were apprehensive, their heads hanging as they stared at the pavement. Black-uniformed SS men were walking ahead and behind, to make sure nobody slipped away.

A few yards back, being kept at a distance by the SS, were the children's mothers, distraught and sobbing. They had suffered for more than three years under the German occupation and they knew better than to accept the glib assurance that their children were being taken away 'for the sake of their health' and would be returning after a month – another cruel euphemism.

Malgorzata Twardecki, like most of her compatriots, had already endured a terrible war. In 1939 she had been living close to the

German border with her husband, an army captain serving as a frontier guard, and their infant son Alojzy. But that year her husband was sent away to the war and she would never see him again: he disappeared, along with three million other Poles. She was alone in the house with Alojzy when the Germans marched in and set fire to her house. She fled on foot with Alojzy until, after about a mile, a farmer on a horse-drawn cart picked them up and took them to her parents' smallholding near Rogozno, some sixty-five kilometres away.

She had lost her home and all her possessions and she had no idea where her husband was. Her first priority was to find a job so that she and the child could be fed. Here she was lucky, for she was better educated than most and spoke reasonably good German. She obtained a clerical job at the district courthouse.

After some months she and her parents were expelled from the smallholding, which was given to a German family. They moved to a smaller house close to the town centre. Before long the occupying Nazis were busy sorting out the inhabitants of the town into racial groups before deciding how to dispose of them. Malgorzata's family qualified as ethnic Germans in that they had German antecedents, and could speak both German and Polish, although they regarded themselves as Poles. Had they wished, they could have signed forms renouncing their Polish nationality to become Germans, and Malgorzata's immediate superior at the court, an ethnic German, urged her to do this. She refused. 'I am Polish,' she told him. 'I am not a German. What I was born, so I will remain.'

Today, in her eighties, she does not regret her youthful defiance; indeed, she is rightly proud of it. Nonetheless, she knows that had she gone along with her boss's suggestion she would almost certainly have avoided the trauma of the next ten years, which was to dominate and nearly destroy her life.

In the summer of 1943, Alojzy was five with blond hair and bright blue eyes, tall and advanced for his age: he had walked at nine months and was talking on his first birthday. He was Malgorzata's only child and, in the absence of her husband, her life revolved around him. One morning a policeman knocked on her door and told her she must take her son to the district council office for testing. When she asked what they were being tested for, the policeman replied ominously: 'They are taking all the children away on holiday, for their health.'

'My child is quite healthy – he doesn't need a holiday,' she protested, trying to hide her mounting fear. 'He is my only child. I am not letting him go.' Yet she knew she had no choice but to obey the summons.

There were between one and two dozen mothers at the council office when she arrived. The children were examined medically, their heads and chests measured, the colour of their hair and eyes solemnly recorded. There was never really any doubt that the fair-haired Alojzy would pass muster, for he represented just the stock the Third Reich needed. Malgorzata was told to take him home and await instructions.

Two weeks later the order came. She was to have Alojzy at the council office by 6 a.m., with enough clothes to last him four weeks. He was going to be sent, with other children from the town, to a 'sanatorium' for a 'holiday'. It was an instruction couched in the terms of an offer, a familiar Nazi tactic. She knew only too well what it meant – that however much she may have wanted to, she would not be allowed to refuse. Like the other mothers on the list, she was frantic. None of them believed that the children would return in four weeks: they knew enough of the Nazis and their inhumanity to doubt that they would ever see them again.

So Malgorzata did not take Alojzy to the office at the appointed time. While she knew she had almost no chance of escaping the edict, she clutched at every straw. At 7 a.m., inevitably, a military policeman knocked on the door to say that if she chose not to take him herself, the child would be forced to go along without her. The policeman allowed her time to get Alojzy dressed. At the council office the children were separated from their mothers by uniformed SS men, who arranged them into ranks for the march to the station. They did not go through the station building but passed to its right and walked straight on to the platform, where they were met by a group of the notorious Nazi nurses known as the Brown Sisters. A train, billowing steam, was already waiting to take them away.

The mothers were allowed nowhere near the platform. Police with dogs confined them to an area outside the station, behind a barrier on the other side of the road. The Nazi mayor of the town was there as well. 'They will be well cared for,' he assured the pleading mothers. 'And it will only be for a month.' Unconsoled, the women wept and wailed, unable even to say one last goodbye. As the train drew out they watched increduously, knowing that there was nothing whatever they could do about it.

Many of our most horrifying images of Nazi oppression involve trains; indeed, it is hard to imagine how they could have imposed their particular brand of terror had it not been for the railways. The cattle-trucks taking Jews and others to the concentration camps are the best-known examples, but the entire policy of wholesale removal of populations from one territory to another, in Poland and elsewhere, would have been virtually impossible to put into effect without this efficient and easily policed form of mass transportation.

The mothers watched the last billow of smoke dissipate as the train faded into the distance, then they drifted home without their children but with, instead, a terrible feeling of emptiness. They had lost their children and there was no way of getting them back. Fifty years later, standing on the station platform, Malgorzata cried: 'You can't imagine what it is like to have a child stolen. We didn't give them our children, they stole them. Such a thing has never happened before. My mother told me that in her lifetime she had seen wars – the French war and the First World War – but nobody had ever done anything as terrible as this.'

Because she could scarcely credit the barbarism of what had happened, Malgorzata's mother at first tried to console her. 'Don't take it so badly,' she counselled. 'They may come back after all.' Malgorzata knew they would not but a mother does not give up hope and so, when a month had passed with no news of Alojzy, she went to see the mayor.

'Where are the children?' she asked. 'You said it would only be for four weeks.'

'Get out,' the Mayor replied. 'Get out before I kick you out.'

Word filtered through that the children had been taken to the centre at Kalisz, between the cities of Poznan and Lodz, now serving the purpose envisaged in the directive from the Interior Ministry the previous December. Malgorzata discovered that there was a miller in Rogozno who regularly delivered flour to Kalisz. She asked him if he would take her there and he agreed. But she came too late. Two days earlier, she learned, the children had been taken from Kalisz; possibly for the very reason that the mothers had discovered where they were. The older ones had gone to Austria and the youngest, including Alojzy, to Germany.

Alojzy had not been quite alone on the journey from Rogozno to Kalisz. Among the older boys in the group was his eleven-year-old cousin Leon Twardecki and Leon's friend Jan Tloczynski. Because the older boys were better aware of the true nature of what was being inflicted on them, they were more upset than the younger ones and several were in tears. Despite his apprehension about his own fate, Leon felt responsible for his cousin and, as the train chugged first to nearby Poznan, then east through the monotonous flat landscape, he sought to comfort him as best he could.

When they got to Kalisz they were taken to what Leon thought from its appearance was a convent. He was right that it had been one – and it is again today – but during the war most of the nuns had been removed, to be replaced by SS race office personnel and the Brown Sisters. The children soon realised that, far from being on holiday, they were at what amounted from their point of view to a boarding school. To begin with Leon and Alojzy were allowed to share a room and after their first night – and still more medical tests – they were taken to classrooms for intensive lessons in the German language and about the Nazi version of history. Although the place was more thoroughly policed than any conventional boarding school, they were allowed to spend most of their time together and even occasionally to go for supervised walks around the town.

There were other things going on at Kalisz that they could not have known about. The results of their 'medical' tests were being analysed meticulously, using long and detailed forms on which sixty-two separate physical characteristics were carefully noted and classified as being typical of a racial group. Important pointers were the colour of hair and eyes, thickness of lips, height and posture (true Germans were thought to sit erectly, while the Slavs were hunched up). The shape of the nose was such a vital factor that it was assessed in two parts, so that a child's nose could be categorised as being Jewish at the tip but Aryan where it met the face.

After the results had been noted, each child was placed in one of eleven racial categories, from the highly desirable Aryan specimens to the lowest of the low. Those who exhibited the characteristics of many different races, or only of the 'inferior' ones, were placed in the bottom categories. Children in the top three classifications – in other words those wholly or predominantly Aryan – would be eligible for adoption by childless SS or Nazi couples, where they could be assured of a comfortable and ideologically correct upbringing. Those in the middle rank would go to less politically committed couples, or families who had some children already.

Nobody much minded what fate befell those in the lowest categories: the long-term aim was that they should be eliminated entirely from the Reich, by the end of the century at the latest. In the meantime many went to concentration camps or the special children's camp at Lodz where, in the Nazi scheme of things, it did not matter how or even whether they survived.

The children, of course, were quite ignorant of these life-or-death decisions being taken about their fate. Nor did those who passed the tests know that all records of their birth and true origins were being systematically obliterated. New documents were prepared on which they were allotted Germanised names – Alojzy, for instance, became Alfred, and Leon Leo, while both boys had their surname altered from Twardecki to Hartmann. Like many of the name-changes, this was a species of pun: the literal translation of the Polish Twardecki is 'hard man', so that is what they became in German. Their birth certificates now stated that their mothers had died in childbirth and their fathers had been killed in the war. Their registered birth-dates were altered, too, in case anybody should try to find them at any time in the future.

One morning, about six weeks after the group from Rogozno arrived at Kalisz, a Brown Sister woke Leon early and ordered him to get dressed.

'What about Alojzy?' he asked. 'Aren't you going to wake him too?'

'Let him sleep,' said the woman. 'We don't need him yet.'

Leon realised that he was going to be taken away before his cousin. Disobeying the order, he woke Alojzy.

'They're taking me off somewhere,' he whispered. 'Here, have this.' And he pressed into the small child's hand a religious medallion that had been hanging round his own neck. The two would not meet again for ten years.

Leon, with Jan and the older boys, was taken back to Kalisz railway station. They were not told where they were going and they were frightened. In the event their train steamed south, on a long, winding route through the Tatras Mountains into Czechoslovakia, then to Austria, ending up at Gmunden at the head of Lake Traunsee, east of Salzburg. They were taken to a newly opened training centre, named Alpenland, under the auspices of the Hitler Youth movement, specifically designed to help the *Ostkinder* (children from the East) assimilate with their conquerors.

The Poles and other 'foreigners' were billeted with German boys of their own age so that they quickly learnt the German language and the German way of doing things. They were made to march and sing Nazi songs with the others and were punished if they dared speak Polish among themselves, for German was to be the language of Europe's future and there was no point in clinging on to the quaint regional tongues of the discredited past.

Alojzy, or Alfred as he now was, did not stay at Kalisz for long. With others of his age he was sent to the Lebensborn home at Bad Polzin in Pomerania, north-east Germany. Known as the Pommern home, it was one of the oldest of the Lebensborns, opened a few months after the first one at Steinhöring. Alfred was five and a half when he arrived there towards the end of 1943 – an age when learning and forgetting both come easily. Very soon he was speaking nothing but German, and the Lebensborn authorities were seeking adoptive parents for this bright, blond, blue-eyed boy, whose papers now officially declared him to be a German orphan.

In March, Alfred celebrated his sixth birthday at Bad Polzin. Not long afterwards he received a visit from a friendly woman from Koblenz, in the Rhineland, south-east of Cologne. She talked to him for a long time and he was almost immediately drawn to her. More important, she was bowled over by him. As soon as the formalities could be completed, Margarete and Theo Binderberger, a married couple with no natural children, became his official mother and father. Herr Binderberger came to Bad Polzin to collect him and they travelled on the slow, crowded overnight train, south to Koblenz.

Late the next afternoon Alfred had his first glimpse of his new home, a comfortable house with a large garden which his new parents shared with Margarete's mother and father. In a state of enormous excitement, he bounded through the front door and was delighted to see bowls of summer flowers everywhere. It was all so different from his memories – fading rapidly day by day – of his old home in Poland, where such pleasant luxuries had never been in evidence. Almost the only similarity between the two homes was that, by coincidence, both his 'mothers' had the same name.

Margarete and her parents were there to greet him, his 'grand-father' wearing a green apron – a sight Alfred would soon get used to, for the old man spent a lot of time working in the garden. The grand-father inspected him, turning him round to get a view from all angles.

'Yes,' he declared, after assessing the lad for a short while. 'Yes, he is well built. He will be a fine specimen.' Even at his young age, Alfred found something degrading about this treatment, as if he were a prize bull at an agricultural show. He said he was tired and asked if he could go straight up to bed.

Very soon he developed a loving relationship with his adoptive mother, although he was never close to Herr Binderberger, who earned his living as a skilled engineer with the arms manufacturer Krupp. He was a member of the Nazi Party – this was why Margarete had her pick of the 'orphans' at Bad Polzin – and an army reservist who had to go for training one evening a week. After Margarete, Alfred's closest relationship was with her father, who was honoured as the head of the family. A Prussian with a bristling white moustache, he was a former officer in the Kaiser's army, who disapproved of Hitler because he had only been a lance-corporal.

Alfred fitted in easily at the local school because he now spoke German with scarcely a trace of a Polish accent. He made plenty of friends. They were all, naturally enough, absolutely committed to the German side in the war and convinced that the Fatherland would emerge victorious. They idolised Hitler and over Alfred's bed hung a picture of the Führer in his Reichsmarshal's uniform, his officer's cane pointing towards the east. Koblenz was a garrison town and officers were often visiting the house – especially from the air base, where Margarete had a job.

Towards the end of 1944 Herr Binderberger was called up to fight on the western front. As the end of the war loomed the family spent more time in the air-raid shelter beneath the house and everyone – even the children – was given a protective helmet. One morning Alfred woke up to find American soldiers in the streets, spilling from trucks and tanks with white stars on the side. White flags were hanging from the windows of all the houses. He wept and, like the rest of his family and friends, blamed the communists for the cowardly decision to surrender. Not long afterwards his adoptive father came home from the front. Almost the first thing he did was to tear Hitler's picture from above his son's bed and take it up to the attic. 'You traitor!' Alfred shouted at him – and was spanked for his patriotism.

When the Americans left, the French army replaced them as the occupying power. As a former party member Herr Binderberger could not expect any favours from them and the family were ejected from their house. The five of them found accommodation in the house next door, but only in three rooms, compared with the ample space of their former home. Yet they were a loving, mutually supportive family and, once the immediate shock of the defeat had passed, Alfred continued to enjoy a happy childhood.

Back in Rogozno, now that the war was over, Malgorzata Twardecki, like thousands of other Polish mothers, began the search for her son. It was hard to know where to start, for the Nazis had done an effective job of covering their tracks. She wrote to the occupying powers in all four of the zones into which Germany had been divided, sending photographs and asking for news. Bombarded with thousands of similar requests from all over Europe, and absorbed in the overwhelming task of seeking to restore some sort of normality to a shattered and demoralised nation, the Allied administrators did not know where to begin. Usually they would send form letters in reply, promising to let the supplicants know if they had news. They scarcely ever did.

About a year after the war ended, Leon returned to Rogozno. He had been relatively easy to repatriate because he had never been adopted, but was still in a Hitler Youth camp when the Americans (fortunately including some of Polish extraction) marched in. Since he had been ten when he was taken he could tell officials precisely where he came from. Those of Alfred's age and younger, who had been taken into loving families, had no such recollections: they thought of themselves as Germans, and were proud of it.

Because Leon's father was dead and his mother terminally ill, when he got back to Rogozno he went to live with his Aunt Malgorzata, and gave her a useful clue as to how to pursue the hunt for her son. It was, he said, no use looking for someone named Twardecki: both their names had been changed to Hartmann. (He did not of course know of the further change of Alfred's name to Binderberger.) This was a joyful moment for Malgorzata, a sudden onset of new hope. Despite her show of dogged determination, she secretly despaired of ever finding her son again. All her letters and enquiries had come to nothing. But now Leon arrived with a piece of new information which could prove critical. Filled with fresh optimism she sent another barrage of letters to the authorities.

Still she drew blank after blank. Then someone advised her to contact members of the Polish mission in Berlin who were, after all, on the spot, and had access to those Lebensborn files that had not been destroyed by the retreating SS or the Americans. Some months later, in the spring of 1947, she received a reply: her son's name was now Binderberger and he was living with adoptive parents in Koblenz. The mission sent her the address and added that, if the adoptive parents raised no problems, Alojzy could be home within months. She was overjoyed. After four years, here at last was firm news. She wrote to the Binderbergers in Koblenz.

Malgorzata's letter came to the German family like a bolt from the blue. They had never been given an inkling that their son Alfred was Polish and their first instinct was simply not to believe it. Their reply was polite but unyielding. Alfred, they insisted, was a German orphan and there was no possibility that he was Polish. Apart from anything else, he *looked* so German. While they appreciated the difficulty of tracing Polish children, given the chaos in Europe when the war ended, they wrote that in this case she had clearly been given false information. They would not entertain the thought further.

The desperate mother, her new-found hope suddenly dashed, persisted. She wrote to Konrad Adenauer, the West German Chancellor, but did not receive a reply. She sent the Binderbergers a picture of herself and of Alojzy as a child but they refused at first to admit any resemblance. She continued to write. Most of her letters were ignored and when an answer did come it was not from the adoptive parents but from Margarete's mother and father, who intercepted most of the letters in case Alfred should see them.

When the Polish mission sent representatives to the house to ask to see the boy, the Binderbergers would say he was not there, that he was staying with a relative in another town. The Western Allies and the postwar West German Government did not help Malgorzata, for although they still paid lip service to repatriating displaced persons, they were not, with the Cold War now firmly in place, going to make any very determined efforts to send children back from the Western sphere of influence to the communist East. In the worsening international situation, humanity was quickly giving way to *realpolitik*.

Yet Malgorzata's pleas, although still being rejected by the family, were having a cumulative effect. The seeds of doubt were sown in the Binderbergers' minds. Maybe Alfred was Alojzy after all.

One day in 1949 the eleven-year-old Alfred walked home from school as usual with his friend Peter Holler. It had been a good day and, after waving Peter goodbye, he whistled to himself as he bounded up the stairs to the cramped apartment. As he opened the door to the living room, though, he stopped in his tracks. His parents and grandparents were sitting there solemnly, as if forming some kind of reception committee. They sat straight in their chairs, like a stiff family group from the early days of photography. His father had a letter in his hand, and began speaking straight away.

'Alfred,' he said solemnly, 'we have been waiting for you. This is a letter from your mother.'

'But Mother is sitting next to you!' Alfred exclaimed, thinking it must be some elaborate joke that he would soon understand.

'No, this is from your real mother. She lives in Poland.'

Nobody said anything for a few moments. Then Herr Binderberger began to explain what had happened in the occupied countries during the war, how children had been kidnapped from their homes and their true origins concealed. He told the boy that, when the first letters came, they had refused to believe Malgorzata's story, but now they thought that, given her persistence and the photographs she had been sending, it was probably true.

When his father was finished Alfred stayed silent for a while. It was all too much to take in. To think he might be Polish was the most shattering blow of all because, like all German children, he had been fed with the persistent Nazi propaganda line that the Poles were an intrinsically inferior race, worthy only of doing those manual jobs that were too degrading for pure-born Germans.

He had come across some during the war, those that had been taken to Germany as slave labourers. They were unshaven, often unwashed, and looked desperately ill. Sometimes they wore newspapers tied round their feet instead of shoes. They would do odd jobs such as carrying coal for the family, and his father would hand them out cigarettes as a tip. At school, 'Polack' was a term of abuse, as in phrases such as 'lazy as a Polack'. Yet now he was being told that he was one of them. Not for a minute would he begin to believe it.

Alfred began to cry. Herr Binderberger gave him the photographs of his Polish mother and of himself as a child, and a letter addressed to him. 'Dear Alojzy,' it began.

'I'm Alfred, Alfred Binderberger, not Alojzy,' he shouted, before reading on:

> My dear son,
> I wonder if you realise that I have been trying to get you back home ever since 1947? Surely you remember your cousin Leon and the day you were both taken away from Rogozno to Kalisz by the secret police? Leon has already come back through the International Red Cross. Your grandfather died in 1948, but don't you remember how you used to creep up when he was nodding in the chair and pull his hair? Your grandmother was 80 last November. She asks whether you remember how you used to go shopping with her and pull at her skirt until she bought you lemonade. I beg you as my son to write me a few lines and send me a photograph of yourself. I can't wait for the time when I can press you to my heart.
>
> Your loving mother and grandmother

Alfred threw the letter down angrily. 'I'm not going to have anything to do with her,' he insisted. Then he tore up the letter and the photographs, threw them into the wastepaper basket, stormed to his room and flung himself on to his bed, sobbing.

In the emotional turmoil of the ensuing days Alfred decided that, even if the story of his parentage was true, he had no intention of being reunited with his natural mother. He was happy in Koblenz. Nor did the Binderbergers make any effort to persuade him otherwise. He was, after all, *their* only child, too. They loved him and gave him almost everything he wanted. They could hardly sympathise with his natural mother – if that was really what she was – for many women had suffered equally heavy losses in the horrors of the war. Poland was now part of the Eastern bloc, firmly entrenched behind the Iron

Curtain, and all the reports reaching the West spoke of the hardships that its inhabitants had to endure. The Binderbergers had no doubt at all that, by nearly every measure, it would be in the best interests of the eleven-year-old boy to stay where he was.

The following year, though, Alfred and the family suffered a heavy blow. Margarete was diagnosed as having cancer and became progressively more ill, at one time spending almost a year in hospital, in agonising pain. She was the person Alfred loved more than anyone else in the world and her obvious suffering upset him deeply. It affected his performance at school and he was kept back in the same class for a full second year.

Herr Binderberger was a caring father but he had never been as close to Alfred as either Margarete or the grandfather. Not long after Margarete's death he married her cousin. Alfred disliked the new Frau Binderberger and the feeling was mutual. He quarrelled increasingly with her and, as a consequence, with his father. The atmosphere at home was tense and, in the summer of 1953, it was arranged that he should go to spend the school holidays with some of the grandfather's relatives in England, from a branch of the family that had emigrated there before the First World War. The idea was that he should learn English and perhaps eventually study at a British university.

Not long before he was due to go, another letter arrived from Malgorzata, inviting him to spend the summer holidays with her. It happened that, on the day it came, he was in the throes of one of his frequent arguments with his father. To spite him as much as anything else, Alfred said: 'All right, I won't go to London. I'll go to Poland instead.' He was convinced that Herr Binderberger would veto the plan but, to his great surprise, he acceded to it readily. 'Fine,' he said. 'I'll buy your ticket tomorrow.' Alfred instantly regretted his rashness, but he had backed himself into a corner from which he could not escape without losing face.

He told hardly any of his friends where he was going, because he had not confided in them when suspicions about his origin were first raised. He just assured them he would be back in good time for the start of the autumn term. On a fine July morning he loaded his precious blue bicycle – a present for his four-teenth birthday – on to the family Volkswagen and climbed in for his father to drive him to the station. His grandfather waved from the front door; and as they drove away Alfred had a sudden premonition that he would never see either of his grand-parents again.

The train was immensely crowded, with scores of people standing in the corridors. It passed into the Eastern zone of Germany where he saw his first Russian soldiers, armed with Kalashnikovs. His first port of call was Berlin, where he had to get a visa from the Polish mission. In the week it took to process, he stayed with the Polish consul and his family where, for the first time that he could remember, he heard Polish spoken.

When the visa came through he was taken, still with his bicycle in tow, back to the station and shown into a sleeping car, where the Polish attendant was asked to keep an eye on him. After a while Alfred, now getting increasingly on edge, became irritated by the thorough way in which the attendant was fulfilling the instruction, popping his head into the compartment at regular intervals. It made him feel under surveillance, as he had on the day he had arrived at Koblenz, when Margarete's father had inspected him so offensively.

The real reason for his unease, though, was his deep apprehension about what he would find in Poland. All he had heard about it was that it was very cold and consisted mainly of forests, where bears and wolves roamed; that the people lived primitively in houses heated by wood-burning stoves, and were averse to washing. He did not recall – although as an infant he must have been told – that it had once been a kingdom and that it had produced great writers, composers and scientists who had won Nobel prizes. Half in earnest, he conceived a plan. As soon as he had greeted his mother at Poznan station he would say that he now intended to return directly to Koblenz.

When Malgorzata received the letter from Koblenz telling her that her persistence would soon be rewarded, she could scarcely contain her feelings. The previous year she had taken a second husband, an old friend from the town who had known Alojzy as a child. Determined to be on the platform when her son arrived, she insisted that they took the midday train from Rogozno to Poznan, although the train from Berlin was not due until late at night. A wait of around ten hours was nothing in the context of the ten years she had already spent longing for this moment.

She and her husband stationed themselves at both ends of the platform but at first, in the bustle of the arriving train, with doors slamming and excited cries of recognition all around them, they could see no sign of the boy. Then Malgorzata spotted a tall, lone figure climbing slowly down the steps from a carriage. 'That's him!' she shouted, and rushed towards him. 'It can't be,' said her husband, following behind her. 'He's so tall!' In his mind he had pictured someone not very much older than the five-year-old that Alojzy had been when the Germans took him. Moreover, in his smart clothes and short, neatly combed hair, he looked typically German. But Malgorzata had no doubts. 'That is him,' she insisted. 'I would recognise him anywhere. He looks just like his father.'

She approached the boy and held out her hand. 'Alfred Binderberger?' she enquired. He took her hand. He had been dreading this moment, when an emotional middle-aged woman he did not know would, he was certain, sob uncontrollably and throw herself all over him. All Malgorzata's instincts, on seeing her only son for the first time in ten years, were to do precisely that, but she understood instinctively that any such melodramatic gesture would unsettle him. By an extraordinary effort of will, she held back the tears welling inside her.

'Good evening,' she said. 'I hope the journey wasn't too bad.'

Alojzy had by now abandoned his former plan to go straight back to Germany. Instead, he said: 'I have only come here to look around and to find out if it is all true. I shan't be staying very long.' He looked hard into his mother's blue eyes. She did not reply directly to his statement of intent, but smiled and nodded and introduced him to her new husband who, although himself feeling the emotion of the occasion, kept urging Malgorzata to stay calm.

On the train journey to Rogozno an incident occurred that brought home to Alfred and his mother the problems he would face if he were to decide to stay in Poland for good. In the compartment was a Polish officer. Alfred had never before seen a uniform like it and stared intently. As he did so, he noticed a dark stain on the front of the man's tunic. 'In Germany,' he told his mother, 'an officer would never be seen wearing a dirty uniform like that.'

He spoke in German – the only language he knew – and he spoke loudly. He was not being deliberately provocative but, having lived in Germany since the end of the war, he had no idea of the depth of the anti-German feeling that existed in Poland, nor indeed of the dreadful atrocities that had provoked that feeling. Eight years after the defeat of the Germans, the Poles still resented them deeply and hated hearing their language. Many, however, understood it, and a few began shaking their fists at this brash youth – a German so far as they could tell – who was criticising one of their soldiers. The officer turned to Alfred and addressed him in fluent German.

'You must excuse me,' he said. 'I have been travelling for three days non-stop.'

Alfred's stepfather interceded to ease the tension in the carriage by explaining the position – in Polish – to the other occupants. Suddenly the hate on their faces disappeared, to be replaced by a mixture of wonder and goodwill. Alfred, who had come back to his native land prepared to decry and scorn everything and everyone he encountered, found his attitude mellowing slightly.

Another lesson came when he arrived at his parents' flat. It seemed surprisingly warm, comfortable and welcoming. But the fact that it was lit by gas confirmed his preconceptions about the primitive conditions he would be living in. He walked quickly through the three small rooms, apparently searching for something.

'What are you looking for?' his stepfather asked.

'The wood stove,' he replied.

His stepfather laughed. 'You must be thinking of Russia,' he said. 'That's even further east.'

Alfred's first days in Rogozno were lonely. He could not speak to others of his own age because of the language – and he did not bother to try learning any Polish because he was, after all, returning to Koblenz in a month's time. He spent most days cycling by himself, exploring the surrounding countryside – and because it is quite flat he could cover long distances. Defiantly, he had brought with him a pennant carrying the German flag, and flew it on the bicycle. Occasionally, children would throw stones at him.

On the credit side, he was growing ever closer to his real mother. Her gentleness and understanding reminded him strongly of the much-missed Margarete. Naturally, she treated him like a prince, seeking to make up for the lost years. He was spoiled and humoured as much as he had been by his German mother just after he had arrived from the Lebensborn home. He was still, though, convinced that Germany was the superior country and was looking to find fault. Malgorzata told us that at dinner one evening he complained of a hair in the milk pudding – so his stepfather took the pudding bowl and poured it all over his head.

Alojzy, as he was now being called again, remembers differently from his mother the circumstances in which his planned four-week holiday turned into a decision to stay in Poland for good. He recollects that about halfway through the month he came in from a cycle ride to find his mother crying. He asked her why and she said it was because he would have to go back to Germany in two weeks. On impulse, to cheer her up, he said: 'I'll stay' – but without really meaning it. His mother reacted with such joy that he found himself bound by the commitment, as he had been when he told his German father that he would spend his holidays in Poland.

Malgorzata, by contrast, recalls that what sparked the decision was a letter from Herr Binderberger asking him whether he really wanted to go back to Germany, and urging him to think seriously about staying with his natural mother. Alojzy assumed this was due to the influence of his father's second wife – and it was indeed only because of her that he gave the suggestion any consideration. He went into his room to re-read the letter. Coming out, she recollects, he said: 'Mama' – the first time he had called her that – 'Mama, I'm going to stay. But I shall have to go to school and learn Polish.' Recalling that moment more than forty years on, Malgorzata, her eyes shining, said: 'I felt born again.'

Both these affecting but conflicting memories leave out the most important practical reason why Alojzy stayed in Poland: the authorities would not let him leave. In 1953, the year Stalin died, tension was high in eastern Europe and the Cold War was building to its peak. There was an unsuccessful rising in East Berlin against communist rule and, the following year, the Russians would reject Western proposals for German reunification. All this meant that controls over population movements were at their height and visitors to all countries in the Soviet bloc were obliged to register with the authorities. Alojzy went to the control bureau not long after he arrived and was made to give up his German passport. 'Come back in a week,' he was told. 'You will get it back then.'

The following week he went back to the control bureau with his mother. There he was given a form to sign, but as it was in Polish he did not understand it. Malgorzata said nothing, so he signed it and asked for his passport.

'What passport?' the official replied. 'You are now a Polish citizen. You have just signed a form to confirm it. And you are not allowed a passport.'

That meant that he was unable to leave Poland to travel to Germany or anywhere without special permission. When he asked for permission – as he did every year for the next six or seven years – it was routinely refused, presumably because the authorities feared he would not come back. He had, in effect, been kidnapped for a second time. For sixteen years he was unable to go back to the place he remembered as home, not even for the funeral of his German father. He was thirty-one by the time he saw Koblenz again in December 1969.

Today Malgorzata and Leon still live in Rogozno. Alojzy, married with a family of his own, lives in Warsaw, where he is a college lecturer. He believes that his fractured childhood has taught him a number of valuable lessons:

I was a German nationalist. I came to a country that has always been seen by Germans as the enemy, and that has in the same way always seen Germany as *its* enemy. I had to find a *modus vivendi*. Today I regard myself as a patriot both of Poland and of the Rhineland. How can you be a nationalist if you have both a Polish mother and a German mother?

Once at an exhibition in Dusseldorf I saw a sculpture that I would have bought if I could have afforded it. It showed a man sitting between two chairs and holding on to them both. I said: "That's me." Most important, I have learned that there are no sub-humans and there are no superhumans.'

7

Children of Poznan

> Our task in the next century, as it was in the olden days, is to reinstate Nordic man as the leadership class, the universal aristocracy that rules the world ... If we find a person here [in Poland] of good race we want to take his child and bring him to Germany. If the child does not reconcile himself to this we must kill him, because as a potential leader he will represent a danger to us. If he is reconciled we shall rear him amongst us and never let him come back here.
>
> *Himmler addressing SS officers in Poznan, Poland, November 1943*

Poznan, on the flat plain midway between Berlin and Warsaw, has a history of being a focal point for Polish nationalism. Its citizens resisted an earlier attempt at Germanisation before the First World War. A popular uprising in 1918 forced the Germans to quit, freeing the city to join the new Polish state. The rebellious tradition continued after the Second World War, when in 1956 food riots in Poznan forced the Russians to loosen their grip on what was effectively a client state.

Small wonder, then, that after the German occupation of 1939 the city should have been a hotbed of resistance. One of the most important underground fighters was Franciszek Witaszek, a bacteriologist at Poznan University. He was an expert in poisons and used his knowledge to kill first of all the horses of the occupying German forces, then, by spiking their food, a group of senior SS officers. Some months after the series of mysterious deaths he was betrayed and arrested in April 1942. He was executed in January 1943, when his head was severed and put on display before being sent to a research centre in Germany, where it was recovered after the war; it is now buried in the heroes' cemetery in Poznan, which contains an impressive monument to him. The rest of his body was never recovered. In the same month his wife was sent to Auschwitz, then to Ravensbrück, where, against the odds, she survived.

The couple had four daughters and a son born in 1942. When, following Francisczek's arrest, the police came to take away the mother they also took the two smallest girls – Alodia, who was five, and Daria, two years younger – because both had striking blonde hair. They were sent first to the racial bureau in Poznan, where they underwent the first of the standard racial tests. Then they went to stay with relatives until September, when a fleet of lorries arrived to take about a hundred selected children on the first stage of their journey to Kalisz to begin the Germanisation process. To this day, that morning is so engraved on Alodia's memory that she remembers the large black boots worn by the SS officers and she can even recall what she herself was wearing – a bright red coat with matching bonnet. With her, she carried a small case of clothes and treasured possessions. As the lorries drew away, the children's parents and guardians ran alongside it, howling with anger and despair.

The children were not taken far, just to a transit camp on the outskirts of Poznan, to await space on the increasingly crowded trains. A few days later the lorries returned to take them to the station, where they were put in cattle-trucks and taken to the children's camp at Lodz. There they spent between two and three months, undergoing still more tests, with more photographs, and learning the rudiments of German before moving on to Kalisz.

Conditions in Lodz were harsh. Autumn was quickly turning into a chilly winter and they were not given adequate clothes. Some children died and several began to wet their beds. Those who did so were taken outside and hosed down with cold water, then beaten. Since bed-wetting was regarded as a sign of congenital weakness, they would lose their chance of being placed in the top racial categories, which meant that ultimately many would be disposed of.

Alodia and Daria were lucky in that they were at least able to share a room for their entire time at Lodz. At Kalisz, though, Alodia became seriously ill with diphtheria and was taken to a local hospital for a throat operation. There she was in a public ward and worked out a plan to get herself free – a cunning ruse for a child of her age. She told other adults visiting the hospital that she had an uncle living not far away and persuaded them to contact him so that he could come and take her away. The uncle visited the hospital and bribed staff there to allow her to leave with him. It was all fixed – but before the plan could be put into effect she had been discharged from the hospital, returned to the Kalisz camp and, in January 1943, dispatched with her sister Daria to the Lebensborn home at Bad Polzin.

Conditions there were better than at Kalisz or Lodz – the rooms were comfortable and there was an expansive garden. But the rules were still rigorous: the punishment for speaking Polish was a beating. Their names were changed to Alice and Dora Wittke and after three months both sisters, by now fluent in German, were ready to be sent for adoption.

Alodia first met her German mother in April 1943. She was the wife of a German soldier who had been taken prisoner by the Allies. When she visited the home to choose from among the children she was immediately attracted by Alodia's looks and the feeling was mutual. Those children who came from loving families were missing their mothers badly, and were in a mind-set where they would fall for almost anyone who showed even the smallest shred of concern for them.

The prospective mother, Frau Dahl, came to the camp and took Alodia for a walk to get to know her. As they were walking, Alodia spoke of her sister also being at the home and Frau Dahl immediately offered to adopt her as well, rather than break up the already depleted family. But she had reckoned without rigid Nazi officialdom. It was a strict rule that children should be separated from their siblings, as part of the process of obliterating all memories of their former home. So despite Frau Dahl's pleas, Daria had to stay at Bad Polzin and watch her elder sister being driven off to her new home at Mecklenburg, some sixty kilometres north of Berlin.

In the ensuing months Frau Dahl, urged on by Alodia, repeatedly tried to trace Daria, but the Lebensborn staff refused to give out any information. After the war the family discovered that Daria had spent another month at Bad Polzin before being sent to an Austrian family who treated her as a young domestic servant. Alodia, by contrast, was lucky with her German mother, a loving woman who doted on her.

In May 1945 Alodia's Polish mother arrived back in Poznan from Ravensbrück. Her war had been horrendous but at least, unlike so many of her compatriots, she had survived. Now she hoped she could partly make up for the lost years by recreating a family life for herself and her children. She had received no definite news of her husband but she guessed that, given the nature of his offences, he probably would have been executed by the Nazis and she had prepared herself mentally for that blow as best she could. The appalling truth was quickly confirmed to her – and then the bottom fell out of her world for the second time when she was told that her two daughters had been kidnapped.

Like Malgorzata Twardecki, she wrote scores of letters to the authorities to trace the children, and similarly met the problem that their names had been changed and all records destroyed. She was in despair until finally the indefatigable Dr Roman Hrabar, who made a career of reuniting Polish families severed by the war, hunted them down in 1947, cracking the code by which Witaszek had been changed to Wittke.

When Dr Hrabar succeeded in tracing Polish children he had learned to expect two contrasting reactions from the German adoptive parents. 'It depended on their psychology,' he recalls. 'Usually they didn't want to lose their children and they would hide them when we came. They were desperate to keep them. But the best of the German parents would realise that they had to do what was best for the children and let them go home.'

Frau Dahl had no inkling that her daughter Alice was Polish until she was contacted by the Red Cross. When she found out it was a shattering blow, but her reaction was that of the good parent, the precise opposite of that of the Binderbergers in Koblenz. Much as it grieved her to part with the cheerful little girl, she accepted that it was right that she should go back to her natural mother. In November 1947 she took her to Berlin and put her on the train to Poznan.

It was an agonising time for her but, unlike so many consequences of these disastrous historical events, it had a surprisingly happy outcome. When they met after Alodia had gone home, her German and Polish mothers struck up an immediate rapport and got together a number of times before Mrs Dahl died in 1971. It was a remarkable friendship. By any logic the two women should have been sworn enemies, rivals for the custody of the same child, whom they both loved deeply. Yet humanity and tolerance triumphed over all the obstacles that stood in the path of a warm and ultimately close relationship. Mrs Witaszek died in 1984.

For part of her life, therefore, Alodia had the benefit of two mothers, but that scarcely made up for the fact that she was never able to enjoy a normal childhood in Poland. At first, as she spoke no Polish, children of her age naturally assumed that she was a German, one of their hated tormentors. Although she had been happy with her German mother and reluctant to leave her, she was greatly looking forward to meeting her long-lost brothers and sisters. Imagine her disappointment at discovering that she could not communicate with them at all. Even when she relearned her native tongue, she still spoke it with a noticeable German accent.

Daria, who returned from Austria a month after Alodia got back, was in the same position, and the two girls therefore formed a close relationship. But they were confused about their identity. Who and what were they, Polish or German? So disappointed were they with their homecoming that, a few months after their return, they sneaked off to the railway station together in the hope of jumping on a train back to Germany. They were quickly caught and sent home. 'For us,' Alodia reflects today, 'the war went on for ten years, not five.'

If you bear left when you come out of Central Station at Newcastle-upon-Tyne, in north-east England, and keep ahead at the roundabout, passing the Roman Catholic church, you will be on Westmorland Road. As you climb the steepish slope the environment deteriorates. You pass petrol stations and run-down terraces with video stores and small newsagents. There is a modern college building away to the left but everything else has a windswept and bedraggled look – the kind of area you would not want to linger in unless you had to.

Father Alexander Michelowski does have to. Near the top of the slope, adorned with the Polish crest, is a sombre grey building, stiff with locks and bars to protect it against vandals and intruders. It is the Roman Catholic chapel and social centre of Newcastle's small Polish community. Father Michelowski, who runs the chapel, has his office and a tiny studio flat at the rear. If it seems an odd place to come and look for victims of the Nazis' racial policies, it does symbolise the dislocation that the policies were created to engender, and did.

The Gestapo came for Alexander Michelowski six weeks short of his eleventh birthday, on 28 May 1942, a month after they had taken Alodia and Daria Witaszek. He was the eldest of four children. His three sisters were out when the uniformed men jumped out of a lorry in front of the family house in a Poznan suburb, pushed open the door and rushed in wielding rifles. 'Hands up or I shoot,' one of them said, while another grabbed Alexander and bundled him into the lorry, where scores of other children from the neighbourhood had already been collected. They were told that some of them would be going on a free holiday, and each carried a small bag of clothes.

They were driven to a nearby children's home run by nuns, where eleven doctors – ten men and a woman – were waiting to inspect them. They were made to stand on a table, then strip to the waist and sit in a chair, around which the eleven doctors stood in a circle, each with a detailed printed form on which they scribbled notes and placed ticks to denote how the child measured up on the sixty-two key physical attributes. Each examination took only a few minutes. When the last child had been seen, the chief doctor read out a list of names of the children who had passed the test – about sixty, perhaps half the total group. The rest were sent home.

Although he was rather small for his age, Alexander was one of those chosen. He and the others were taken to the station for the train to Kalisz. On the platform he was approached by a pleasant-faced middle-aged woman in ordinary street clothes. Looking round hastily to ensure that nobody was listening, she whispered that she was the Mother Superior at a convent near Poznan, but was not wearing her habit because the Germans wanted to arrest her. She gave him a picture of the Black Madonna of Czestochowa, Poland's most potent religious symbol, reputed to have been painted from life by St Luke. 'May the mother of God protect you,' she said, before vanishing into the crowd.

Alexander was already very attached to the Catholic faith and was an altar-boy at his church. He vowed that he would keep the picture with him, along with the prayer book from his first communion, whatever terrors the future might bring – for after two and a half years of living under German occupation he had no illusions, and knew better than to believe the story that they were going on holiday. During the next three years in German institutions he would cherish the picture, going to great pains to keep it concealed from the Germans and even from his fellow captives. Today he believes fervently that it was due to the Madonna's protection that he emerged from the war alive. His belief in its powers was certainly a constant source of comfort to him; a crutch and a symbol that, one day, the bad times would end.

Soldiers escorted the group on the train to Kalisz, where they were taken by lorry to a place Alexander immediately recognised: it was a convent where his aunt had been a nun. All the nuns had been expelled, though, and the place, surrounded by walls, was being used as a Germanisation centre for Polish children. When they arrived they were stripped, given baths and issued with uniforms of the Hitler Youth movement. Their own clothes and their luggage – which in Alexander's case included his Bible and Black Madonna picture – were taken away and placed in an attic. A few days after their arrival he went up there, removed the two precious objects and stuffed them inside his mattress.

One incident from the first few days is still imprinted on Alexander's memory. Although the Nazis had kept the children's destination secret from their parents, one mother had discovered where her son, aged five or six, was being held. She entered the convent and, seeing the child in the playground, shouted his name while rushing up to embrace him. A Gestapo guard, hearing the commotion, ran to her and knocked her to the ground, where he kicked her until she bled. As she lay wounded on the ground the guard picked her up and threw her over the convent wall. To this day, Alexander does not know whether she lived or died. That night in the dormitory he and his friends discussed the incident and vowed that from that moment they would not co-operate with their captors any more than they were compelled to.

'We all vowed to get even,' he remembers today. 'We would avenge that Polish mother.'

The days at Kalisz were spent learning German and going on long marches, when the uniformed children were made to sing Nazi songs. Conforming with their standard practice, the Germans changed their names: Alexander Michelowski became Alexander Peters. Then in July, a few days after Alexander's birthday, they went on a long train journey of two days and nights to the Oberweiss Castle on Lake Traunsee in Austria, near the camp that Leon Twardecki would be sent to some months later.

The children at Oberweiss were all Polish. Here the regime of marching, singing and learning German was more intense than at Kalisz. If they were caught speaking Polish, they were made to go without food for twenty-four hours. Even as winter drew in, they were not allowed to wear anything more than the regulation thin shirt, shorts and sandals, and they suffered agonies from chilblains. As they marched up and down the five-kilometre road to the nearest town of Gmunden, sympathetic bystanders would throw warm clothes to them, but they were not allowed to pick them up.

The older boys, of whom Alexander was one, remained defiant and devised ways of flouting the stern rule of their SS guards. One of the boys was always detailed to help out with the shopping, and whoever it was would try to steal food from the shop while the order was being collated. Perpetually hungry, the boys would arrange post-midnight feasts in the dormitories after the guards had gone to bed. Here the stolen food was consumed, as well as milk that they had taken from the store in the cellar. This ruse was uncovered when, in the darkness one night, Alexander did not realise he had spilt milk all the way up to the dormitory. In the morning it was easy for the guards to follow the trail to his bed, and he was badly beaten for the offence.

At these late-night banquets the boys would discuss plans to escape. They made three attempts while Alexander was there, using the classic device of hanging knotted sheets from windows. They had to be careful to conceal their plans not just from their guards but from the girls who occupied the next dormitory, whose reliability they doubted. Despite these precautions, at the first two attempts they were betrayed by a 'trusty' and caught before they had left the grounds; but the third time they managed to get as far as the surrounding hills, where they camped for the night until they were sniffed out by tracker dogs in the morning.

One rather more successful ruse involved overcoming the embargo on mail. They were not supposed to send or to receive any but some of the children had managed to let their families know where they were being held. Any letters addressed to them at the home would be intercepted even before they reached the local post office, but the boys were lucky enough to find a sympathetic Polish woman living on a farm near the castle. Their initial contact with her had been fortuitous. They had been taking fruit from the trees at the farm when one of them saw her coming and shouted a warning to the others in Polish.

The woman was surprised to hear her native tongue and asked them what Poles were doing in that part of Austria. They told her their story and, when she seemed sympathetic, they asked if she would help them with their mail problem. She agreed to let them use her farm as a cover address. The postmaster was persuaded to co-operate and would hold back mail addressed to them at the farm until one of the boys, at considerable risk if caught, found an opportunity to collect it. Alexander had not managed to make contact with his own family in Poland, but nor had many others, so he was not too worried. In any case, he had more immediate problems to grapple with, such as keeping warm and nourished.

The official plan for the boys was that, once they had perfected their German, they should be placed for adoption with the right sort of Austrian family. Older boys were more difficult to place than either younger children or girls, and Alexander was one of eleven in his group not claimed. The initial selection procedure, as he recalls it, was like a slave market, with the children parading for inspection by prospective parents. He had in fact been chosen by an SS family but they never came to pick him up.

In the autumn of 1944 the six eldest out of the eleven unplaced boys – those coming close to their fifteenth birthday – were sent off to join the German army. The other five, Alexander among them, were to go to a Hitler Youth camp at Maria Schmoll in the southern part of the country. Escorted by German soldiers, they were placed on a train, but by this time the Allies' final assault on Germany and its satellites was well under way and travel was extremely hazardous.

The American Air Force was making low-flying bombing and strafing raids over that part of Austria, using the formidable Flying Fortress aircraft, mounted with machine-guns. The train carrying the boys was strafed and they were forced to jump out and take what cover they could find beside the tracks. The attack damaged the line so that the train could not continue, and the officers accompanying the group decided that they had no option but to proceed on foot, although their destination was a two-day walk away. They spent the night sleeping in a haystack.

The most direct route to Maria Schmoll was along the railway track, but this made them vulnerable to more strafing from the Flying Fortresses. Alexander is convinced that he owes his life at this point to the skills of the German officer escorting the group – those and the protection of his Black Madonna picture. The officer taught them to wait until the planes were quite near and almost had them in their sights, then quickly to throw themselves to the ground. Since the gunners could not swivel their weapons to fire directly below them, this manoeuvre would protect the group from the most dangerous few seconds of the onslaught. There were several close calls but the whole party survived.

About one thousand members of the Hitler Youth were camped out at Maria Schmoll in tents, each of them accommodating fifteen boys. The new Polish arrivals were split up – two in one tent, three in another – to discourage them from speaking Polish among themselves. It was essentially a military training camp, for by this time, after D-Day, it was clear to the German High Command that they were going to need every young man and woman they could muster if disaster was to be avoided. The boys underwent basic weapons training and yet more strenuous route marches.

In November 1944, with the German hold on the territory becoming ever more tenuous, the boys were told that they would be evacuating the camp the following day. They were given emergency rations of three biscuits to sustain them during the evacuation, in case no more substantial food supplies were available. Alexander had a premonition that the biscuits would not be needed, for he guessed that the American troops were closer at hand than the camp commanders knew, or at least than they cared to admit. Because of his perpetual hunger he ate one of his biscuits as soon as it was handed to him – and was beaten for his lack of restraint. He encouraged the others to do the same, though, convinced as he was that the rations would not be needed.

His premonition proved accurate. At dawn next morning they all heard the boom of anti-tank guns and the crack of machine-gun fire, as the American tanks, with white stars on their sides, rolled towards them and, behind the tanks, parachutists dropped from the sky. White flags fluttered from all the houses in the village and there was scarcely any serious German resistance. By lunchtime the camp was in American hands and most of its inmates were Allied prisoners.

Alexander explained to an American officer that he and his four friends were not German but Polish, and that they had in effect been imprisoned by the Germans. It would, he argued, be quite unfair if they were to be detained again, this time by the other side. After testing them to prove that they really were Polish, the occupation authorities agreed that the five should be treated differently from the German members of the Hitler Youth. They were sent to a variety of refugee camps and given Polish lessons so that they could become fluent in their language again, after years of being forbidden to speak it.

Shortly after the final German surrender in May 1945, Alexander found himself at a camp quite near the Oberweiss Castle on Lake Traunsee, where he had been held by the Nazis. From discussions with American officers about his own future, he knew that the question of repatriating Polish children taken by the Germans was already causing concern to the occupation forces. He suggested to the American administrators that he should return to Oberweiss to see if there were any documents there that might give the addresses of parents who had adopted or otherwise taken charge of the children. They agreed. He was given an American uniform and was driven to the castle by an officer in a commandeered Volkswagen.

When he got there he asked for the SS officer who had formerly been in charge of the home but was told it was now a children's hospital. In the kitchen, he recognised a woman who had been a cook when he was there, but she said she knew nothing of any records. Then Alexander remembered that a woman who lived quite near the castle, who used to come and help out in the German language classes and was married to a policeman, had adopted a friend of his named Helena, about a year younger than him. He remembered where she lived and the American officer agreed that they should drive there.

Alexander did not want to be the first to enter the house, because both the woman and Helena would have recognised him. He described the girl to the officer, who went in on his own. After a few minutes he came out again. 'There's a girl there that answers your description,' he told Alexander, 'but the mother says she's a German orphan and she has papers that seem to prove it.'

Alexander explained that these papers were customarily falsified, and suggested that they should go back into the house together. 'She will recognise me,' he assured the officer. 'You will see what will happen.'

As soon as Helena saw Alexander she smiled, while her adoptive mother turned pale and refused to speak. Helena confirmed that she was in fact Polish and the officer told her to go and pack. Alexander warned him that the woman's husband, the policeman, might cause trouble and it would be better to take the girl away before he returned home.

While they were waiting for her to pack, though, Alexander was suddenly seized by doubt. Were they really doing the right thing? What if they couldn't find Helena's parents in Poland – perhaps they had disappeared like so many others. Even in these early days of peace, it was clear that the future of Poland, as of all the East European countries liberated by the Russians, was going to be uncertain. Perhaps Helena would have been better off staying in this rather pleasant part of Austria, with a couple who were clearly fond of her and seemed to be looking after her well. Still, it was too late for these second thoughts now.

When Helena returned, carrying her small bag of things, she turned to say goodbye to her adoptive mother, but still the woman stood silent, her eyes glazed in venomous anger and frustration. Alexander and the officer took the girl to the car and started the engine. Suddenly the woman, sobbing furiously, dashed from the house, jumped on to the car bonnet and began pummelling the windscreen with her fists. At that very moment her husband arrived on his motor-bike. Seeing Helena in the car, with the two men in American uniforms, the policeman sized up the situation, helped his wife down from the car and took her in his arms to comfort her, accepting there was nothing he could do to stop the girl being taken away. In December 1945, Helena was reunited with her parents near Lodz.

For Alexander himself, the future was less straightforward. He had not heard a word from his parents or his sisters since leaving Poland. He made contact with his grandfather and an uncle who gave him terrible news: there had been a massacre soon after he left and his immediate family were assumed to have perished in it. The tragic story was not unique, for many millions of Poles have never been accounted for following the carnage and chaos of that dreadful period.

Despite this disaster, it would have been open to Alexander to return to Poland and it would in many ways have been the obvious thing to do. He would have certainly found somewhere to stay while he re-established his life: indeed, the parents of one of his four Polish friends from the Hitler Youth camp, who had come to Austria to pick up their son, had offered to take Alexander back with them. But by this time he already felt a strong vocation for the priesthood. He believed that Providence may have decided that he could do God's work more effectively outside his native country. In a sense, his faith became his home. And the Americans, although they were not preventing anybody from returning to Poland, were not actively encouraging those who had no remaining close family ties.

Those who expressed no wish to go back were divided into groups and sent to other countries. Initially Alexander went to a camp run by the Polish armed forces at Arco, near Verona in Italy. When the army group went to England in 1946 he travelled with them.

'We were welcomed at Dover with brass bands and crowds of people who gave us food parcels,' he recalls. 'It was a terribly cold winter. First we went to Conway in Wales, where the gales howled all night and we didn't have enough blankets. Then we were moved to Norfolk which was just as bad. There was no water because the pipes were frozen – I remember having to wash myself with ice.'

After attending a humanist college he enrolled in the Polish Navy School at Landywood, near Wolverhampton, later moving with it to Oundle in Northamptonshire. Then he went to France to begin his religious training, joining a missionary order for Poles in exile. After three years in a French seminary he studied for six years at the International University. He was ordained in 1961 and then went back to England, where he has remained for most of the time since. Beginning with the Polish community in Balham, South London, he has been a priest for exiled Poles in Dunstable, Blackburn, Lincoln, Southampton and, most recently, Newcastle.

In the 1970s he went back to Poland for the first time since the war. It was an extraordinary, emotional and in some ways disorienting experience. He had been old enough when he left to retain quite vivid recollections of his childhood there, but after the devastating conflict and the thirty years of communist rule that followed it, there was very little that was familiar, no landmarks that he could use as an anchor to recreate the images of the pre-kidnap years.

There was one important thing he wanted to do. He felt he must assuage the doubts that had plagued him for more than a quarter of a century about Helena, the girl he had helped remove from her Austrian adoptive parents. Had he, after all, done the right thing? He tracked her down to an address in Lodz and called there one afternoon. When he rang the bell a small girl answered, only a year or two younger than Helena had been when he last saw her. She said her mother was at work at the courthouse, where she was a judge.

'Phone and tell her that Alexander has come to see her,' he said. 'Tell her I'm an old friend from the camp in Austria.'

As soon as she could, Helena left the court and rushed home. After the tears and the talk, as they caught up on what had happened to them since they last saw each other, Alexander plucked up the courage to put his crucial question: 'There's one thing I must ask you. Did I do the right thing when I took you from that Austrian family by force?'

Helena smiled. 'It was the best thing you could have done,' she replied. 'I know I might have had a more comfortable life if I had stayed in Austria but here I have been able to live and grow up at home with my own family. I always wanted to be a lawyer and today I am not only a lawyer but a judge. My Austrian family would not have given me the same education.'

It is impossible to say how many Polish children were taken from their families by the Nazis, but it is certain that only a small proportion were returned. Thousands are living in Germany today, many of them unaware of their origin. In June 1948 the Polish newspaper *Zycie Warszawy* stated that, despite the efforts of the government in Warsaw, 200,000 Polish children were being prevented from returning home by the West Germans and the Western occupation authorities. Apart from children taken for Germanisation, that figure also includes children born in Germany to those 'sub-human' Poles sent there as manual labourers. The article was especially hard on the British, whom it accused of wanting to hang on to the Poles to send out to their overseas colonies.

While there was an element of propaganda in this report, it was certainly true that the Polish Mission in Germany, which had the responsibility of arranging for the children to be repatriated, received less and less co-operation from the occupying powers. The Polish official in charge of repatriation efforts was Dr Roman Hrabar, who worked with the fledgling United Nations and other refugee organisations. He recalls how hard it was to prove that a child was Polish, when its memories of its early life, its language and its relatives had been systematically expunged by the Germans.

Even when a child's identity had been established beyond doubt, Dr Hrabar quarrelled many times with the occupation authorities about the desirability of repatriation. Often they would cite humanitarian motives for wanting a child to stay put in Germany, although Dr Hrabar suspected a political motivation:

> I remember a colleague in the British zone saying that it would be a new crime to take this child from a family where it has already been living for a long time, and to force it to get used to another new father and mother. I argued that one day the child would grow up and would learn that its real parents were living in another country, and this would cause psychological problems. But sometimes the foster parents would agree to give a child up if we could show them that the real parents were alive and were desperate to have their child back. And in some cases the child has benefited by keeping in touch with both families. A lot depends on the psychology of the child and both sets of parents.

Usually, and quite naturally, there was fierce resistance from the adoptive parents when it was suggested the children should go – as in the case of Alojzy Twardecki and his German parents. Sometimes the children would be moved out of the family house and hidden in another town so that the authorities could not trace them. Yet even when children were returned, their reunion with their natural parents at the railway station was often a shock and a disappointment to both sides. Some children were unable to recognise mothers whose physical appearance had been altered by the ravages of war. Sometimes, unless the mothers spoke German, they had no common language in which to talk. This was, after all, precisely what the Nazis had intended.

Yet if it was Himmler and his accomplices who had masterminded this calculated deconstruction of family ties, the victorious Allies, ironically enough, helped ensure that the Nazi aims were partially achieved. Just as the Germans placed their national ambitions above any concern for human suffering, so did the Americans, the British and the French let the prosecution of the Cold War come before the interests of bereft Polish families. Unwittingly following Himmler's precept about not presenting your potential enemies with the gift of future leaders, they placed a low priority on sending Polish children back to the East. As so often in the past, the Poles were assigned the role of victims.

Because of all the obstacles in the way of repatriation, fewer than 40,000 Polish children went back from Germany and former German territories after the war – about a fifth of the estimated total of those taken. Dr Hrabar fears that, despite the horrors and personal tragedies that stemmed from this fatally misguided attempt at racial engineering, the lesson may still not have been learned.

'We see radical National Socialist movements in Germany again today,' he says. '*Mein Kampf* has become a new kind of gospel for many groups. If we want to avoid genocide in the future, we must understand what happened in the past.'

8

Maids of Norway

This is a Germanic people, so it is our duty to educate its children and young people to make the Norwegians a Nordic people again, as we understand the term. It is definitely desirable that German soldiers should have as many children as possible by Norwegian women, legitimately or illegitimately.

> *SS Lt-Gen. Rediess,*
> *German High Commissioner for Norway, 1943*

The German national film studio at Potsdam was part of the Nazi propaganda empire of Josef Goebbels, but not all its films were designed to deliver a knockout political punch. Some were purely escapist and certainly *The Star of Rio*, completed in the first weeks of the war in November 1939, falls into that category. A trashy black-and-white musical about a jewel theft, it contains only two clues as to the cultural climate of the time: the idealised Aryan features of the heroine, La Jana, and the distinct Tyrolean overtones which intrude into the Latin American rhythms.

It is surprising that there is a market for the video of such an undistinguished film, but Werner Thiermann is glad that one has been made. A Norwegian truck driver, retired early through ill-health, he has lost count of how many times he has sat in front of the television at his home in Farstad, on the rugged coast of Norway, and watched the film from beginning to end. It is not that he is a particular fan of German 1930s musicals, or indeed anything of a film buff at all. What keeps him watching is the hope that one day he will spot something that until now he has missed – some conclusive evidence as to the identity of his father.

Thiermann is one of many thousands of Norwegian children born to local women and members of the German army of occupation between 1941 and 1945. His search for his father has consumed much of his life, and he now carries out family research for others in the same situation. He has become convinced that, before the war, his father was a bit-part actor at the Potsdam studio, and that *The Star of Rio* was one of the films he appeared in. Thiermann has been told by members of the actor's family that he might have been playing the part of a policeman; but there are several policemen in the cast. Werner Thiermann freezes the video when they appear and studies their faces, hoping to spot, in a distinguishing feature or even just a fleeting grimace, the tell-tale family resemblance.

On 2 April 1940 Hitler invaded Norway without warning and very soon the Germans were in full control. The Norwegians were no match for them militarily, and an attempt by Britain to mount a counter-invasion was a disastrous failure. Although the Norwegian fascist leader Vidkun Quisling was nominally Prime Minister, real power lay in the hands of the German High Commissioner, initially Lieutenant-General Rediess, Hitler's personal representative. Himmler, in his role as Commissar for the Consolidation of German Nationhood and as the controller of the Lebensborn movement, was excited by the prospect of a mass transfusion of high-calibre Norwegian genes into the German racial stock. Ebner wrote to him suggesting that racially and politically valuable Norwegian women should be brought to Germany to breed, and Himmler agreed enthusiastically:

> The compulsory transfer to Germany of Norwegian women expecting children by German occupation troops is a unique opportunity. It would be in accordance with the objective of transplanting purely Nordic women to Reich territory in large numbers. There is a special need of 'Nordicisation' in south Germany.

Of all the European peoples the Norwegians are the most Nordic, with their blond hair, statuesque appearance and their physical toughness, manifested in their skills as seamen and their ability to withstand the extreme conditions of the Scandinavian winter. The purity of their blood-lines could scarcely be matched even by

Heinrich Himmler, who saw the Lebensborn homes as central to his plan for producing a master race.

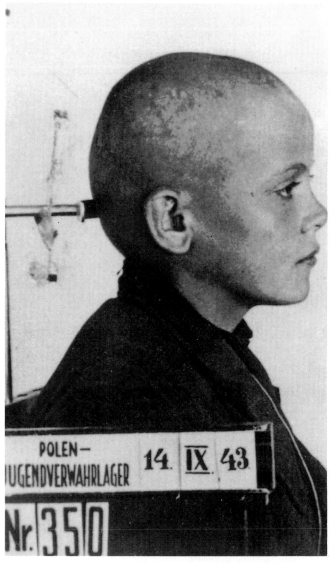

POLEN—
JUGENDVERWAHRLAGER 14. Ⅸ 43

Nr. 350

A child has his head measured to determine his racial characteristics. He is labelled as coming from Poland on 14 September 1943.

(*above*) Suitable prospective "parents" examine a line-up of children for adopting and fostering.

(*below*) An unusual racial testing document, showing 21 physical characteristics to assess and grade from 1 to 5. Three separate assessments are needed for the nose alone: its bridge size, length and width. Bottom left are the 11 racial categories: N for Nordic was viewed as the best and Ng for Negroid the worst.

Name:		Vorname:		Alter:		Formel:		I	II	III	IV
		Männer über 180 Frauen über 170	171—180 161—170	161—170 151—160	151—160 141—150	unter 150 unter 140		Körperhöhe:			cm
1	Körperhöhe	1 sehr groß	2 groß	3 mittelgroß	4 klein	5 sehr klein		Sitzhöhe:			cm
2	Wuchsform	1 schlank	2 mächtig	3 mittel	4 untersetzt	5 dick		Gewicht:			kg
3	Haltung	1 straff	2 aufrecht	3 bequem	4 lässig	5 schlaff					
4	Beinlänge rel.	1 sehr lang	2 lang	3 mittel	4 kurz	5 sehr kurz					
5	Kopfform	1 sehr lang	2 lang	3 mittel	4 kurz	5 sehr kurz					
6	Hinterhaupt	1 ausladend	2 gewölbt	3 mäßig gewölbt	4 flach	5 deformiert		Lichtbild			
7	Gesichtsform	1 schmaloval langrechteckig	2 oval	3 breitoval	4 rund	5 trapezförmig rhombisch		Vorderansicht			
8	Nasenrücken	1 gerade	2 gewellt	3 schwach auswärtsbogen	4 stark auswärtsbogen	5 einwärtsbogen					
9	Nasenhöhe	1 sehr hoch	2 hoch	3 mittel	4 niedrig	5 sehr niedrig					
10	Nasenbreite	1 sehr schmal	2 schmal	3 mittel	4 breit	5 sehr breit					
11	Backenknochen	1 unbetont	2 schwach betont	3 betont	4 vorspringend	5 stark vorspring.					
12	Augenlage	1 sehr tief	2 tief	3 mittel	4 flach	5 vorquellend					
13	Lidspalte	1 spindelförmig	2 weitspindelig	3 mandelförmig	4 geschlitzt	5 enggeschlitzt					
14	Augenfaltenbildung	1 leichte Deckfalte	2 schwereDeckfalte	3 deckfaltenlos	4 Epikanthus	5 Mongolenfalte		Seitenansicht			
15	Lippen	1 dünn	2 mäßig voll	3 voll	4 dick	5 wulstig					
16	Kinn	1 vorspringend	2 ausgeprägt	3 schwach	4 zurückliegend	5 fliehend					
17	Haarform	1 schlicht — wellwellig	2 lockig	3 engwellig	4 kraus	5 straff					
18	Körperbehaarung	1 schwach	2 mäßig	3 stark	4 sehr stark	5 fehlend					
19	Haarfarbe	1 hellblond	2 rotbld. bis dklbl.	3 hellbraun	4 braun	5 schwarz		Bemerkungen:			
20	Augenfarbe	1 blau 1a—2b	2 blaugrau 3—5	3 graugrün 6—7	4 hellbraun 8—13	5 dunkelbraun 14—16					
21	Hautfarbe	1 rosig — weiß	2 fahlweiß grauweiß	3 gelblich	4 bräunlich	5 braun					

N	F	D	W	O	Ob	Va	Or	As	M	Ng	unbestimmbar +	von:

Unterschrift

Druck vorbehalten

(*above and right*)
Children line up
for inspection at
the children's
camp at Lodz,
Poland, where
many of the
stolen children
were taken for
racial testing.

(*left*) Alodia Witaszek and her sister Darya before they were forcibly removed from their home in Poznan by the SS.

(*below*) After Alodia was returned to her natural mother (right) her German "mother" visited her in Poland and the two women became warm friends.

(*left*) The cousins Leon (left) and Alojzy Twardecki, before they were kidnapped together from their Polish village when Leon was 10 and Alojzy four.

(*above right*) Alojzy aged 10, renamed Alfred Binderberger, when he was living with his German adoptive parents. (*below*) Leon today.

(*above*) Malgorzata Ratajczak revisits the railway station where, more than 50 years ago, she had to watch her son Alojzy and her nephew Leon being taken away in a train, not knowing whether she would ever see them again.

(*below*) Alojzy and Malgorzata in Poland today.

Mounted Nazi troops on the lookout for likely Polish children.

Aryan Germany itself, and an infusion of their stock could not fail to enhance the racial health of the Reich. Himmler visited Norway in the autumn following the invasion and discussed with Rediess the best way of exploiting this genetic goldmine. In December Rediess wrote to him with good news – intelligence reports indicated that the Norwegian baby boom was about to begin:

> Though no statistical evidence is yet available because of the short period since the occupation of Norway, there are increasing signs that the friendly relations established by the German occupation troops with local women have made a substantial contribution to the number of births to be expected.

Yet the cautious Rediess pointed out potential problems. Many of the mothers-to-be were already seeking help from the German authorities because, in the anti-German atmosphere that prevailed, they were being 'despised and boycotted' by Norwegians for having given themselves to the occupying troops. If the children were not taken to Germany or properly looked after in Norway, there could be two unwelcome consequences: they might be neglected or abandoned by their mothers or, perhaps worse, they would be absorbed into the Norwegian community as potential enemies of the Reich. Thus all that good German blood, and the exertions of the lusty soldiers, would have gone to waste. Rediess conceded that it could not be expected that the fathers, even if legally free to do so, would make the ultimate sacrifice:

> Only a small proportion of the unmarried fathers conclude from the fact of their paternity that they should marry the child's mother and thus bring mother and child into the sphere of influence of the German Reich. Thus if we no take no steps to care for these Norwegian mothers, we shall increase the numbers of those who oppose German penetration of Norway.

So the strategy was to be that the SS, as in Germany, would take over responsibility for children born in its homes, in effect becoming their guardians. Once satisfied about the purity of their racial inheritance, the German administration would pay an allowance for their keep, either to their mothers or to adoptive parents. Some mothers would be taken to Germany to give birth, in which case the children would be granted German nationality.

Preparations proceeded fast in the first weeks of 1941. Himmler sent SS Major Tietgen, a specialist in racial matters, to oversee the operation. Tietgen decreed that the children of all German soldiers, not just the SS, would be admitted to the Norwegian Lebensborn homes, provided the mothers were racially unblemished and had no record of anti-Nazi political views. To be admitted to one of the homes, mothers were required to sign a declaration that there was no foreign blood in their heritage.

In July 1942 Hitler issued a decree whose effect was to legitimise the Germanisation programme that Himmler and Ebner had already put in place. The decree set the objective of 'the maintenance and advancement of racially valuable German inheritance' by providing 'special provision and care for the children of German armed personnel born to Norwegian and Dutch women'. It allowed for other countries to be included in the scheme later. According to the decree, the German authorities were to meet the costs of the women's confinement, pay a maintenance allowance to the mothers before and after the birth, and accommodate the mothers and children in special homes, with their consent. Mothers were also to be provided with appropriate employment after their babies were born.

The children conceived by Norwegian women and German soldiers fell into several categories. At the lowest level of priority, as far as the Germans were concerned, were those whose mothers maintained good relations with their families and were willing to look after the children themselves in their family homes. Many of these cases were unknown to the German authorities – which is why the official figures of German-fathered children born in Norway during the war, which range between 6,000 and 12,000, are probably an underestimate. The authorities reasoned that if the woman's parents were prepared to accept a German grandchild they were unlikely to express strong feelings against the occupying forces, at least not overtly. The mothers of these children had to undergo no racial test and received no financial support; if, as many would, they turned out to be blooming with racial health, that would be counted as a bonus, a gilt-edged return on a minimal investment.

Next up the scale came the children born in Norwegian Lebensborn homes. Like their German counterparts these children were the responsibility of the SS, who would try, soon after their birth, to have them fostered or adopted by families in Norway sympathetic to the Nazis. The first of the Norwegian Lebensborn homes was opened in April 1942. Luxury villas, hotels and residential institutions were requisitioned for the purpose. Although the Norwegian organisation was technically independent of its parent in Germany, some German staff were sent to help run the homes. Ebner took a great personal interest in what went on in them and in September 1943 paid a visit to Norway. He was not tremendously impressed, pointing out that only one of the homes had a doctor of its own. As a result of his visit, SS doctors and midwives and race specialists were sent out from Germany and central control of the organisation was tightened up.

Some of these Norwegian-born children were sent to Germany soon after birth, without their mothers. Since they were often of more desirable racial stock than children with two German parents, it seldom proved hard to arrange their adoption by a German family. There were suggestions after the war that in some cases this was done without the mothers' permission, but there is no conclusive proof of this, and it was denied at the Nuremberg trials. The Lebensborn authorities were careful to see that the transactions at least had the semblance of legality. In most cases the mothers gave signed permission for their children to be adopted in Germany and Quisling's collaborationist government raised no objection.

Top of the line, by the Germans' reckoning, were the children whose mothers went to Germany to give birth, as Ebner had recommended. Often – but not always – they went because the child's father had agreed to marry them. After these mothers were given language and indoctrination courses at the Kurmark home near Berlin, they would usually live with relatives of their child's father while he was away at war. Preferably they would seek employment on farms, rather than in the cities with all the temptations and potential for corruption that Himmler so abhorred in them. Country life was not compulsory, however, and in 1941 a small hostel was established in Berlin itself for Norwegian women planning to marry Germans.

The mothers were clearly regarded as valuable properties, to be cherished and cosseted. Their travel expenses would be paid by the authorities – using banknotes confiscated from the Bank of Norway – and they would be given free health insurance. Indeed, it is through the records of a Berlin insurance company that the number of Norwegian women who came to Germany towards the end of the war can be ascertained with some accuracy: more than 1,000 in 1943 and about 2,000 in 1944.

The quotation at the beginning of this chapter comes from a booklet by Rediess called 'The SS for Greater Germany – with Sword and Cradle'. It made the specific point that the fathers of the children should be assured that they would not have to assume financial responsibility for their offspring. The SS would take care of it, so as to 'relieve the combatant soldier of worries that might affect his morale'. The intention to marry the woman was certainly not a precondition of fatherhood, and indeed marriage would only be approved if the woman's political attitude came up to scratch, as well as her racial purity. If the father was already married, one option would be 'the soldier adopting the child and accepting it in his own family, as German wives show a great understanding of this situation, and it is also in the best interest of the child'.

Occupying armies always leave a residue of offspring behind them, but the reason for the exceptionally large number of German-fathered births in Norway was that the men were actively encouraged to go forth and sow as many wild oats as they could manage. They were told by their company commanders, on specific instructions from Rediess and from Berlin, to invite healthy young women to the free army cinema shows and to wine and dine them in the best restaurants in town. The men could hardly believe their luck. Here they were, indulging in the age-old prerogative of the serving soldier, but instead of being subjected to solemn health warnings and moral lectures from their superior officers, they were being given the green light. Life was sweet.

And so no doubt it would have remained, even for the women and the resulting children, if the Germans' objectives on the battlefield had been attained as readily and smoothly as their conquests in the boudoir. For Himmler's racial plans depended entirely on Germany winning the war. Without that essential precondition, the thousands of children of the master race, created in this orgy of patriotic promiscuity, were to become a lost tribe, left in international limbo. Disowned by their fathers and often an encumbrance to their young mothers, most of these genetic paragons were now an embarrassment both to the defeated and the liberated nations. For the Germans they were a constant reminder of a national racial obsession that had gone disastrously wrong; for the Norwegians the living proof of how easy it is to slide into easy complicity with a tyrannical and amoral invader.

Not many of the Norwegian children who ended up in Germany were sent back to Norway after the war, partly because they were hard to trace but also because, so intense was the anti-German feeling there, the Norwegians did not want them. According to a report by the International Refugee Organisation in 1947, the Norwegian Government feared that children with German fathers 'might be the bearers of the seed of a new fifth column'. There must be hundreds of men and women in their fifties, living in Germany today, who do not know that their mothers were Norwegian. (Some of the mothers, though, did retain sufficient parental instinct to want their children back. An advertisement in a Berlin newspaper in 1947 sought information about seventeen Norwegian children believed to be with German foster parents. It is not recorded how many were found.)

One child who was returned was a girl named Turid, born in a Norwegian Lebensborn home in 1942 and adopted by a Munich couple in 1944. In this case her Norwegian mother did not want to be reunited with her, but when a refugee organisation traced the girl in 1948 she was taken back to Norway and adopted there. Like several of the children of such parentage, she discovered her true history only when she was getting married and needed a birth certificate. She traced her German adoptive parents and visited them in 1986, but never found her natural mother or father.

Until quite recently the children, desperately seeking to confirm their identity as they reached adulthood, would be confronted with silence, evasions and seemingly insuperable obstacles. That is why Werner Thiermann, who was one of them, has devoted part of his life to breaking down the barriers that were preventing him and thousands like him from coming to terms with their heredity.

The war had been over for forty years before any concerted attempt was made to gain recognition of the right of these victims to discover as much as they could about the individual circumstances of their birth. The campaign began in 1985 when Pier Meek, frustrated in his attempt to identify his father, appeared on television and made a plea for the wartime birth records to be opened up. The response from fellow victims was extraordinary and within a year an organisation had been established with two hundred members, among them Thiermann. In response to the pressure the Norwegian Government began to grant limited access to the archives in 1986, and opened them completely two years later.

Thiermann soon discovered, from his work on his own history, that he had a talent and a liking for such research, and began to help other people with theirs. Today he runs a one-man agency from his home in Farstad and has helped solve more than one hundred cases.

'People decide to look for their fathers when they have seen something on television about the children of German soldiers, or when someone has told them about the work I do,' he says. 'I have such a reputation that when the Red Cross come up against a brick wall they get on to me.

'Usually when people approach me they have very little information. They know where their father served in the war and they think his name is such-and-such but they aren't certain. Sometimes they can find the name from the birth records here in Norway. I have to ask them to be as precise as they can because the German army authorities won't respond to generalised inquiries.'

Thiermann's research tools include a full set of German telephone directories, a book with details of all 88,000 units of the German wartime army, and pictures of regimental badges. Sometimes the enquirers will have a dog-eared photograph, acquired from their mother, of a man they think may be their father. Thiermann can usually tell from the badge on the hat or shoulder what unit he belonged to.

In many cases he finds that the fathers are dead, either killed later in the war or simply of old age, for they would all now be in their seventies. Those who are alive react in different ways when approached. Often they refuse to respond at all; the war was traumatic for the Germans and, in the closing years of their lives, they may be anxious not to reopen memories that they had confined to the backs of their minds. Sometimes, though, the reaction is the precise opposite. A Munich man wrote to Thiermann to thank him for having traced his daughter. A former military official, he had been to Oslo many times on NATO business since the war, and tried to find his child, but the Norwegian authorities had refused to help him.

Some enquiries come from those privileged children whose mothers had been sent to German Lebensborn homes. One of them, who had been adopted soon after birth, wanted to trace her natural parents after discovering the truth, and went to Thiermann for help. His investigation showed that her father, a German officer by then dead, had made a written request to the Lebensborn authorities that his child should be born in Germany and brought up as a Nazi, so the mother had been sent to Germany from South Norway. After the birth the father wanted to marry her but she refused, saying he was too old. The girl was adopted and well looked after and today she has a good job in a bank. Thiermann could not find her mother, who had emigrated to Australia and changed her name, but he was able to introduce her to her three half-sisters. Like many of the war babies who have at last discovered their origins, the woman found a peace of mind that she had lacked before.

Thiermann's investigations throw an intriguing light on to many aspects of this formerly clouded area of twentieth-century history. One wartime soldier was so committed to Himmler's racial crusade that he fathered three children in the space of a couple of months. He made his wife in Germany pregnant before he left home and then, fortified with the knowledge that he was doing his patriotic duty, he seduced two Norwegian women almost as soon as he set foot in the country. Thiermann learned of this heroic odyssey when he was asked by a young man to find his German father. Having discovered the father's name, Thiermann put in his usual enquiries to the army records office, where he was told: 'That's funny, a woman was asking about this man a couple of years ago.'

The woman turned out to be the daughter of the same German soldier. By coincidence, she lived within twenty kilometres of the young man and they had been in the same class at school without knowing that they were half-brother and -sister. The man's mother was still alive and the young woman went to see her. On opening the door to her she exclaimed: 'You must be Leo's daughter. You look just like your father.'

When the Germans marched into Lillehammer in central Norway in April 1940, the residents were naturally apprehensive. The invaders' reputation for cruelty and ruthlessness had gone before them and, although some Norwegians supported the Nazis' fascist philosophy, most were deeply suspicious of extremism of any kind. Yet Astrid Moe, a twenty-eight-year-old divorcée with three-year-old twins, found it hard to work up any strong feelings about the invasion either way. She reasoned that, whatever might befall her under the Germans, it was unlikely to be worse than what she had suffered already without them.

The daughter of a watchmaker, she had grown up as one of eight children in a large house near Lillehammer. The family was respectable and devout. She had been well educated and always did well at school, especially at music: she played the guitar and had a fine singing voice. She also liked to dance, and it was at a dance that she met her husband-to-be. After a short courtship they married, and soon she found herself the mother of twins.

Not long after the children were born, her marriage began to fall apart. Her husband treated her and the children badly and soon he took up with another woman. Most humiliating of all, he brought his new mistress to the family home, sleeping with her in one bed while Astrid and the children slept in another. It was not a hard decision for Astrid to start divorce proceedings. When the Germans arrived, therefore, she was at a low ebb. Her husband was not maintaining the children and she needed urgently to earn some money to feed them. It was small wonder, then, that her first and most pressing thought about the Nazi invasion was that it might provide an opportunity for employment.

Without formal qualifications, she sought domestic work. As one of the first local women to apply to the Germans, she was given a job in the kitchen of Stalag 303 at nearby Joerstadmoen. This was a former army camp which the Germans had converted into an internment centre for Norwegian schoolteachers who were ideologically opposed to the Nazis. (Later in the war it became a prison camp for Russian soldiers and it is today a military communications centre.)

Though poorly paid, the job gave Astrid some security and she found that she got on well with the German soldiers who ran the camp. She was also, like many young and unattached Norwegian women, finding that the men were good company off duty as well as on. Many of the soldiers sent by the Germans to Norway were approaching middle age rather than in their brash early twenties. This was because the High Command had sent its second-league troops to this relatively unimportant outpost, while the higher-profile crack divisions were fighting on the more critical fronts in France and in the east. Being overrun so comprehensively by such a relatively second-rate force was later seen as a source of shame for Norwegians. For the young women, though, it meant that the soldiers possessed a maturity and suavity that they found appealing. Certainly Astrid did, given that her earlier experience with brash youth had been such a disaster.

At a dance in Lillehammer, shortly before Christmas in 1940, she met a German soldier who appears to have told her that he was thirty-three and that his name was Herman. In later years she was reluctant to talk about him, and when she did so the details she gave were inconsistent. It seems likely that he had subtracted ten years from his age and lied about his name. He added that he lived in Berlin and had worked before the war in the film studio at nearby Potsdam.

Astrid was dazzled by him. To someone who had lived all her life in a small Norwegian town, with a population of barely five thousand, Berlin was a city of unimaginable sophistication. Her generation had grown up in the enthralling early years of the movie industry, and going to the cinema was one of the few real treats that Lillehammer offered. Now here she was, dancing with someone who had worked on those glittering sets and met the stars; indeed, someone she might even have caught a glimpse of in one of the German films she had watched. He was kind and gentle – in welcome contrast to her husband – and she fell for him completely. By the spring of 1941 she discovered she was pregnant.

If she was joyful at the prospect of bearing the child of the man she loved, her happiness did not last long. In the first few days of April, as the winter snow was at last beginning to melt, she went to his barracks to tell him the good news. When she got there she was given shattering news: Herman was gone, posted the previous day to northern Norway. Security precautions meant that she could not be given his address, and she never heard from him again.

Once more, she was on her own, with her twins to keep and a new baby coming in the autumn. Her superiors at Stalag 303, who found Astrid more sympathetic and co-operative than many other Norwegian workers, gave her some support. No proper Lebensborn homes had yet been established in Norway but the commander made provision for her to have the baby in the camp's sick-bay, with all expenses paid by the Germans. On 9 October 1941 her son was born there. His birth certificate shows that he arrived in the fortieth week of Astrid's pregnancy and that his racial category was number one – the very best, like prime Scotch beef. In the space on the form where the father's name was supposed to go, the words 'not known' are written. He was christened Hans Werner – two Christian names without a surname.

When the boy was five weeks old he was taken away from Astrid and sent to a children's home that occupied the premises of a former school in Lillehammer. Not officially a Lebensborn home, it seems to have been a makeshift institution, where SS officers inhabited the ground floor and the children were kept upstairs. Because of the strict Lebensborn racial rules, though, Astrid was not relieved of financial responsibility for him. Herman's disappearance had made things difficult for her. Although the baby's birth certificate proclaimed the boy to be of impeccable blood-lines, the rule was that she could only claim child support if the father's racial pedigree could also be shown conclusively to be unblemished. Since she did know where the father was – and the authorities did not know for certain who he was – that condition could not be fulfilled. So for more than a year, on the meagre wage she was paid at the internment camp, she had to pay for bringing up the new baby at the SS home, as well as for the upkeep of the twins who were still living with her.

It was here that her good relations with the German authorities held her in good stead. Early in 1943 the camp's senior officers arranged for her to plead her case in person with no less a figure than SS Major Tietgen, head of the Lebensborn operation in Norway. She was given a train ticket – in itself a rare privilege in wartime Norway – and when she arrived at the station in Oslo a limousine was waiting to drive her to the Lebensborn headquarters. Although she still could not identify her lover positively, she was somehow able to convince Tietgen that he had been a fit sire for an Aryan. Not only was she granted an allowance but, by virtue of a document signed personally by Tietgen, she was to be given 1,409 kröner in lieu of the money she had not received in the first year of the child's life – a substantial bonus, given that her weekly wage amounted to no more than sixty kröner.

With that critical problem settled, Astrid decided to leave Lillehammer, where women who had German soldiers' babies were shunned by the majority of the population. She applied for a transfer and, again through the good offices of the German military, she was appointed to run a soldiers' rest home at Nordseter, a winter sports resort. She was there when the Germans capitulated – but just before that happened she became pregnant by another soldier, and had his daughter in January 1946. The man wanted her to go to Germany to marry him and she accepted the offer, but the Norwegian authorities, then in control again, would not allow it.

From Astrid's point of view, her life and prospects would have been infinitely better if the Germans had won the war, for after it her life never recovered. The local people cut off her long hair – a common punishment for those who consorted with the enemy – and she was imprisoned for three weeks as a collaborator. 'They took everything from her,' says her son Werner. 'Her clothes and everything. I think at one time they were talking about taking the twins away from her. They fined her – and of course they took her pride away. She looked for places to hide, and jobs where she wouldn't have to deal with people. She worked on farms in remote areas.'

Her children, legitimate and illegitimate, found her unwilling to discuss her wartime experiences in any detail. If they sought information about their origins and childhood, she would sometimes sulk for days. On the rare occasions when she could be persuaded to talk, crucial details were often missing or unclear. In 1984 one of her twins died of cancer and two years later an increasingly bitter and demoralised Astrid died, aged 74, as much a victim of the war, in her way, as those who were killed in it.

As they did in Germany, the SS in Norway took great care over the future of the genetically ideal children in their custody. Each potential adoptive parent or foster family would be screened carefully, their homes visited and inspected for hygiene, their political views and records checked out. The complicating factor in Norway was money. Under occupation, the Norwegians were made to endure greater financial privation than people in Germany and, for many of them, the sum paid by Lebensborn for the keep of a foster child was a tempting lure. It was therefore hard to tell whether couples applying to adopt children were motivated primarily by their desire to increase their family and help the war effort, or if they simply wanted to increase their family budget.

Astrid's son, now called by the single name Werner, was taken away from the Lillehammer home in 1942 and, with another baby, fostered on a family in a suburb of the town. Neighbours complained, however, that the couple neglected the children, sometimes leaving them alone while they went out to parties. Lebensborn inspectors confirmed the allegations and found that the children were poorly clothed and fed, the parents pocketing most of the maintenance grant themselves. So Werner was moved back to the home for a while, although sometimes Astrid would have him home for the weekend. In 1944 he was fostered with a committed Nazi family, but that arrangement ended when the Germans left and after the war he was shifted rapidly from place to place. He spent a few months with Astrid's parents, then with her aunt, then with anyone who would agree to take him on for a short time, until he was eventually accommodated at another children's home.

He had no idea of it at the time but, along with the thousands of other Norwegian children of German soldiers, he was the subject of a postwar political wrangle. The Norwegians, now hostile to everything with German connotations, at first wanted to have the children removed from the country. 'I think they regarded us as sub-human,' Werner says. Eventually, after British intervention, a deal was agreed by which the Germans would pay for the children's upkeep in Norway as part of war reparations. Quite large sums of German money were handed over but there is still controversy about how much of it was actually used for the purpose intended.

It was at a children's home, a year or two after the war, that Werner first became aware that his parentage made him different from other children and an object of scorn to many of them. His childhood was dogged by taunts, teasing and occasional physical attacks. One of the first of these occurred at a home where, he recalls, he and a girl, who also had a German father, were shut in a pigsty by one of the staff.

'They let the pigs out of the sty because they said we would make it smell too dirty for them,' he recalls. 'Then when they let us out they scrubbed us down so hard that we went bright pink, and they said that now we looked like pigs ourselves. That was the first time I was told to my face that my father was a German.'

Other incidents followed. Children threw stones and once urinated on him. They would waylay him on his way back from school and to avoid them he would take a circuitous route – only to be beaten when he got home, for being late. When he complained to authorities at the homes where he was staying or at the schools he attended, or even to members of his mother's family, he was generally told that he would have to learn to put up with it, because that was what happened to the children of 'Tyskertoes' – the insulting term used for women such as Astrid, meaning roughly 'German whore'. Being small for his age did not help matters, and the taunting lasted right through his childhood. One day when he was fifteen he was tied up by older boys at his school and assaulted. He reported it to a teacher, who took no action.

Werner deeply resented such treatment and it has left him with an ambivalence towards his native country which remains to this day. 'I was in a way proud of being German because I had nothing else to be proud of, really,' he says. 'I think the Norwegians were so anti-German because they had so much to hide themselves. The people from East Norway, from Trondheim to Oslo, were the worst. Those were the parts that had a lot of Germans in the war. It was the North Norwegians who mostly worked with the Allies.' Perhaps it is not so surprising that such feelings should exist in a country that has given the word 'Quisling' to the English language.

'I've never really had much sympathy for the Norwegians because they haven't given me any reason to have any,' Werner confesses. 'Some of them are still fighting the war in their minds. That's what I find so crazy. They'll never finish with it.'

In 1947 the Norwegian Government, having become resigned to keeping the German-fathered children, advertised in the newspapers for homes for them. 'Blond boys for adoption', the announcements would be headed. They were seeking to place the children with 'good Norwegians', those who had been to Britain or Sweden and had tried to sabotage the Nazis. Werner was taken by a couple in their late forties who lived in Tynset, in the coldest part of Norway. They originally planned to adopt him but in the end they did not. 'They were a little old to be parents,' he says, 'and perhaps I was too wild. I wasn't an easy child to deal with.'

All the same, he was with them for five years, the longest he had ever stayed put in a single place. When he was twelve, Astrid's mother and father took him back for one winter, but in the spring he went back to Tynset. That did not last long because the couple there were not receiving enough money to keep him. They wrote to Astrid asking her to contribute, but she could not afford to. After that he went back for a while to the Nazi couple he had been with at the end of the war; now, nine years later, they had purged their former allegiance and become politically acceptable foster parents once more.

Again, he was quickly on the move, this time because the couple were found to be keeping his clothing allowance for themselves. He was billeted with a churchwarden until, in April 1956, when he was a little over fifteen, he signed up with the merchant navy. After training, he worked on Norwegian ships up and down the American coast. That lasted two years and various short-term jobs followed. For a time he worked as a truck driver in Germany, where he met his future wife, Mary, an Englishwoman from Kippax in Yorkshire. After they married he spent a few years in England, then went back to Norway to do his national service – part of it spent as a seaman on the royal yacht. He wanted to sign on permanently in the navy but an officer told him that his parentage ruled it out. 'We were occupied by you people for six years,' he explained.

He and Mary have had two children but their life has been one of almost constant movement, from one part of Norway to another. They tried Lillehammer for a while but it was too full of painful memories. Then they spent ten years in Tynset. In 1986 an accident suffered while driving a truck injured Werner's back and he had to stop work.

'I've never been able to settle,' he says, 'and I'm sure that's to do with what happened to me as a child. I don't really blame my mother. I've never really thought badly about her, just that she was a person who didn't want to have anything to do with me, although after she died I read some letters she had sent to my aunt saying how I would always be her baby. I didn't understand that. I could never get on her wavelength. There was a wall between us.'

Werner began his long hunt for his father in 1958, when he was seventeen. Effectively abandoned, as he saw it, by his mother, he clung to the hope that his other parent, if he could find him, would provide the roots he craved. For years, Astrid stubbornly refused to give him any information that might help him in his quest, except the name Herman and the name of his unit: the 163 Infantry Division, or the Engelbrecht Division, which had captured southern Norway in 1940. He wrote to the Salvation Army and the Red Cross, both in Norway and Germany, and to the German army records office, but nobody of that name could be traced.

For nearly thirty years that was as far as he could get. The documents that he needed for further progress were sealed, unavailable for public inspection. Then in 1986 the rules were changed and he was finally allowed access to the records of the German wartime administration in the Lillehammer town archive.

Although no surname for his father had appeared on his official birth certificate, SS records suggested that Astrid had told them it was Thiermann, Herman Thiermann. Armed with that knowledge, he wrote to the army records office in Berlin, but they could find nobody with that surname serving in Norway at that time. All the same, relieved at having this one 'fact' to cling to, he had his own name changed officially to Werner Thiermann. Then he acquired a complete set of German telephone directories and wrote to all the Thiermanns in them, asking if they had a relative named Herman. Although he received a remarkable response – about 60 per cent – again he drew a blank.

It then occurred to Werner that the entry on the SS document could have been the result of a mishearing or a misunderstanding. At times of stress Astrid would sometimes stammer, and it was possible that when she said 'Herman' the official had written 'Thiermann'. Perhaps, then, his father's name had been Herman Werner, seeing that he had himself been christened Hans Werner.

In the last year of her life, Astrid had been slightly more helpful in answering Werner's questions about his father. Two solid facts emerged from her memory. The first was the man's earlier career in the film business: she was certain about that. She also believed that for part of his time in Lillehammer he had been batman to a lieutenant named Wagner. When the SS were trying to trace the man during the war they had asked Wagner for the names of his batmen. He said he had two, and added that there was another man in the unit called Herman Heitmann. All three suspects denied having known Astrid.

Through the army records office Werner discovered that Wagner was now dead, but that the head of his unit had been a man named Simmerling, who might still be alive. Werner traced Simmerling through his telephone directories and asked him whether he could remember anyone in the unit who had worked in a film studio. Simmerling came up with three names. One of the men had been shot in Finland when the unit moved there from Norway, the other had been a lighting man, and the third an actor called Ebbers, whose first name Simmerling could not recall.

The army records office could not help with the first two names but they did have something on a Hugo Ebbers who had been in Norway at that time. Born at Gelsenkirchen, near Essen, he had enlisted in 1939 and gone to Lillehammer, but in April 1941 he had been moved to a different unit in northern Norway. This tied in with Werner's father's disappearance as Astrid was about to tell him she was pregnant. In 1943 he was sent to Potsdam – perhaps to appear in propaganda films – and was captured there by the Russians in 1945. In August of that year he was shot. From the German War Graves Commission, Werner discovered that Ebbers was buried at Nardt, near Dresden.

He was now convinced that, at last, he was on to something. The fact that Ebbers was a film actor, and that the timing of his departure from Lillehammer coincided exactly with his mother's memory, was to his mind conclusive. After thirty years of frustration, he was not prepared to let any doubts or possible inconsistencies in the story interfere with his burning desire to believe. As soon as he could, he went to Dresden and placed flowers on Ebbers's grave.

He also wrote to the film studio in Potsdam – which still exists – and there struck more gold. They sent him a copy of Ebbers's wage slip from 1939. This revealed that Erwin Hugo Ebbers was born in 1897 – which would have made him forty-three when he met Astrid, not thirty-three. The slip also included a list of the four films he had appeared in during that year.

Using his phone book again, Werner found an Ebbers living in Gelsenkirchen, who said he was Hugo's nephew. He had been a child during the war but remembered his uncle as a big man in a uniform with stripes. He remembered how proud he had been to have an uncle who had appeared in films. The story in the family was that he had been born Egon Ebbers but changed his name to Erwin Hugo when he became an actor. He was tall, with dark hair and bushy eyebrows – a description that does not fit Werner but does bear a resemblance to his grown-up son.

The next step was to try to get hold of the four films and see if he could spot Ebbers. Even though the name did not appear on the cast list, Werner might recognise a face that recurred in all the films.

From the movie museum at Frankfurt he learned that only one, *The Star from Rio*, was available on video. If he wanted to see the others he could go to the museum and view them there, and one day he will. Meantime, he sits and watches *The Star from Rio* whenever he has a spare moment.

It is a curious form of therapy. Staring for hours at a video, and putting flowers on the grave of a bit-part actor who may or may not have known your mother, amount to a poor substitute for relating to your father; but Werner Thiermann knows that it is as close as he will ever get. He is not planning to change his name again.

Though Norway had far more Lebensborn homes than any other occupied country, Himmler's 'welfare' organisation was active in most of the European nations that fell under Germany's sway. Hitler had personally ordered, in his decree of 28 July 1942, that suitable children from outside Germany should be considered for Germanisation, especially if they had German fathers. Although he singled out Norway and Holland, whose people were notable for their fair skins and general appearance of good racial health, his decree made provision for all the other occupied countries to be included. After the usual bureaucratic in-fighting, Himmler and his SS officers soon saw to it that their organisation should take principal responsibility for putting the decree into effect – except in Holland where the NSV, the Nazi welfare organisation, played the more important role.

At the beginning of 1943 official Lebensborn representatives were appointed in Poznan and Cracow in Poland, Oslo in Norway, The Hague in Holland, and Brussels in Belgium. Although Hitler's decree had placed great emphasis on the role of the mothers, there is some evidence that in practice the aim was to take the best children – i.e. those with German fathers – away from their mothers soon after birth, with or without maternal permission. As Germany's losses on the battlefront multiplied, more and more efforts were made to replace lost men with good-blooded babies from wherever they could be found.

In Holland and Denmark, both potentially fertile fields for Aryan births, hostility towards Germans was much more widespread than in Norway and the Lebensborn programme did not take so firm a hold. There were plans to build a Dutch home for a hundred children and sixty mothers at Nijmegen, near the German border. Inge Viermetz, in charge of the Lebensborn overseas expansion programme, went to The Hague to discuss it at the end of 1942, but it did not materialise. All the same, one thousand children had been born to Dutch mothers and German fathers by the middle of 1943, with the NSV making arrangements for their Germanisation and adoption. Denmark, where about the same numbers of German-fathered babies were being born as in Holland, did get a Lebensborn home, in Copenhagen, but it did not open until the very end of the war in May 1945. After the capitulation it was used as a clinic for women who had escaped from East Germany.

Frau Viermetz also travelled to Belgium to arrange for a small home for twenty mothers and thirty-four children to be set up at Wegimont, midway between Brussels and the German border. Called the Ardennes home, it was to cater for mothers from both Belgium and the north of France, and Frau Viermetz took personal charge of it for a while. The Germans preferred the children of Belgium's Flemish population to those of the French-speaking Walloons, but for fear of alienating the Walloons they did not make too much of this.

The Ardennes home was a constant source of trouble, mainly because of the hostility of the Belgians to the Lebensborn idea, which in turn led to a shortage of suitable locally engaged staff. A detachment of German SS men was sent to provide a security guard on the home, because of fears of possible anti-Nazi attacks. The Germans believed that local hospitals, in particular one run by nuns in Liège, would not treat sick Lebensborn children properly, so they were sent to a German military hospital instead. When one child died at the home, there were suspicions that it had been suffocated by Belgian staff, although the cause of death was later discovered to have been a brain tumour.

When Frau Viermetz returned to Germany she was succeeded as head of the Ardennes home by a Belgian woman who had earlier had her own baby there. She was soon replaced by Major Lang of the SS, but even he could do little to improve the chaotic conditions and poor staff relations. He wrote to Ebner of the 'hostile political attitude' of the Belgian personnel, who, he said, treated the children contemptuously and carelessly. In November 1943, Ebner visited the home and complained about the 'dirt, slovenliness and unqualified staff, some unable to speak German'. Later that month, after a visit by

Sollmann, Ebner wrote to Lang protesting that some of the mothers were giving birth sitting up in a special chair, instead of lying on a bed. 'Women in the home must be delivered on a bed, as they are in other Lebensborn homes,' he ordered.

The Nazis had distinctly ambivalent views about France. On the one hand the French were their natural and traditional enemies, the people who had forced them to grovel for centuries, most recently after the First World War. Their blood-lines had been corrupted by Mediterranean and even North African elements, making many of them, in Hitler's view, suitable only for subjection. But Himmler entertained characteristically romantic notions about the old duchy of Burgundy, which dominated Europe in the thirteenth and fourteenth centuries, when it was a glittering repository of wealth, art, chivalry and culture.

In March 1943 he told Felix Kersten of his and Hitler's plan to reconstitute Burgundy as an independent state run on the heroic principles of discipline, order, tradition – and of course racial purity – which he fostered in the SS. The brave new Burgundy, stretching from the English Channel to the Mediterranean, would incorporate much of its medieval empire, including Artois, Hainault, Luxembourg and Provence, plus Picardy and Champagne. When Kersten wondered what would become of the rest of France, Himmler said it would be turned into an inferior mini-state called Gaul. Although part of the Thousand Year Reich, the revived Burgundy would be a self-governing enclave, a model for other countries seeking to emulate the best Nazi social and racial practice.

That was in the future, though. Before this ideal could be achieved there was the ever more urgent practical objective of capturing the best blood for Germany, as increasing quantities of it were being spilt on the battlefield. Despite his low regard for France as a nation, Himmler recognised that it included some racially valuable elements that could be exploited – the 'Germanic French', as he described them to his Führer when they discussed the question at a dinner in April 1942. Himmler suggested that there should be an annual trawl of the best specimens of such people, 'so that they can be diverted from their accidental French nationality to membership of the great Germanic people, to which their blood entitles them'. Hitler appreciated the twin virtues of the scheme. 'It would be a heavy blow against France,' he said, 'if its leading class was deprived of its Germanic young blood.'

However, France was never an easy country to deal with and there seems to have been no systematic effort to kidnap good-looking French children, as there had been in Poland. Even the fate of children born to German soldiers and French mothers took a long time to resolve. By the middle of 1942, when one estimate put the number of such children as high as 50,000, no attempt had been made to establish a Lebensborn home in France. Himmler instructed that a search should be made for suitable premises and in March 1943 a château was located at Lamorlaye, near Chantilly, to be called the Westwald home. It took almost a year to get it open and the formal ceremony was held in February 1944, although some mothers and children had been in residence earlier. Few of the children appear to have been sent to Germany for adoption. Most stayed with their French mothers and many did not discover their German paternity until much later; in some cases they almost certainly never found out at all.

Ebner visited Westwald soon after it opened and was impressed by the conditions – although not by the SS doctor in charge, Dr Fritz, who insisted on living in Paris, some forty-eight kilometres away, because he wanted to be close to the fleshpots. There were also difficulties with supplies. In May 1944 Ebner wrote to SS headquarters in Paris asking for substantial deliveries to the home of matches, semolina, rice, porridge, cocoa and coloured pencils. In a few weeks the Allies would land in Normandy, so it is unlikely that the provisions were ever sent. By November the home, like the one in Belgium, had been evacuated, and the children sent to Steinhöring.

The only British territory occupied by the Germans was the Channel Islands. Because Himmler had a high regard for British stock, this seemed a potentially productive hunting ground, but because the population was so small there was no major effort to draw on its gene pool until quite late in the war. In 1943 a German commander there wrote:

> Within the Nordic strain of the indigenous population we are dealing for the most part with racially irreproachable children and mothers. In general it can be taken for granted that they

constitute racially valuable material, in contrast with France. These children, and perhaps also their mothers, could contribute to the desired growth of the German population by being settled in the Reich. The position of these unmarried mothers is very bad, as on the one hand they are persecuted by the rest of the civil population and on the other they have been refused any maintenance allowance for the children by the military command in France.

The commander added that many of the mothers had learned German in the hope of being allowed to move to Germany, but most had been refused permission.

In May 1944 the SS race office decreed that the children of German soldiers stationed in the Channel Islands should be racially examined and the valuable ones sent to Germany. Even with their disastrous losses of men on the eastern front, they were still being selective, unwilling to lower standards. The decree added that women expecting German-fathered children should be sent to Lebensborn homes in Germany or France. But before this programme had time to take effect the tide of the war had turned decisively against the Germans and the racial paradise had been indefinitely postponed.

One of the most notorious Nazi atrocities of the war took place at Lidice, Czechoslovakia, in June 1942. The whole village was razed in retaliation for the murder by Czech patriots of Reinhard Heydrich, Himmler's SS deputy leader, who had been governor of the occupied country since the previous year. The village's 192 male residents were shot, along with seven women; the rest of the women – 196 of them – were sent to concentration camps and the 105 children taken away.

Even in the wake of such a brutal act, Himmler made sure that the opportunity to improve the Aryan stock was not missed. On his instruction, the Lebensborn organisation took charge of sorting the children of the village into racial categories. On 21 June – eleven days after the massacre – he wrote to Sollmann instructing him to go to Prague to advise SS General Karl Frank on the question of the children 'whose fathers or parents have had to be executed as members of the resistance movement'. The decision, he wrote, must be 'a judicious one'. The children found to be of no special value would be 'put into camps' – in practice it is believed that most of them were eventually killed. However, the élite were to be spared, for Germany's own good reasons:

> The children of good race, who obviously could become the most dangerous avengers of their parents if they are not brought up correctly and with humanity, should, in my view, be admitted to a Lebensborn children's home for a probationary period where as much as possible should be discovered about their character, then be sent to German families.

The 105 children spent three days with their mothers in nearby school buildings before the women were sent to Ravensbrück concentration camp. After their heads and other features were carefully measured and recorded, the children were sent to Lodz in Poland for more detailed racial analysis. Most of the children had too many Slav attributes to be acceptable and only thirteen of the 105 were judged to qualify for Germanisation. These were sent from Lodz to a Lebensborn home at Puschkau, near Poznan, where they were taught German and the basics of Nazi ideology, before being sent out for adoption.

Only a handful of the Lidice children were traced. Some of them were later to act as guides for visitors to the village, which has been preserved by the Czechs as a monument to the Nazis' vicious inhumanity.

The Lebensborn homes were a Nazi creation and could not survive longer than the movement that gave them birth. In the occupied lands and in Germany itself, they remained in operation as long as they could, until the advancing enemy was only days away. Those in the western territories capitulated first and by the end of 1944 the homes in France, Belgium, Holland and Luxembourg had been closed. The general procedure was for the young babies to be evacuated to homes closer to the German heartland – usually to Wiesbaden – without their mothers. In some cases expectant mothers were also allowed to flee east, but often they were left behind to take their chances with the liberators.

On the eastern front, Bad Polzin was overrun in February 1945 and the children also taken to Wiesbaden, but the following month that home in turn had to be evacuated south-west to Ansbach, near

Nuremberg. The growing band of infant refugees stayed there just four weeks until the remorseless advance of the American army drove them to their final redoubt at Steinhöring. There the Americans found nearly three hundred of them, with a small group of mothers of varying nationalities, when they arrived in May.

Thus Lebensborn ended where it had begun. The Americans, their appointed local administrators and the Red Cross were left, in the short term, to cope as best they could with this curious legacy of a failed experiment in genetic manipulation. The children themselves, plus the thousands of others who had been born or raised in the homes, would spend the rest of their lives coming to terms with their origins. Himmler, whose skewed vision of the world had given rise to the lunatic scheme, poisoned himself when in British custody on 23 May.

9

A Kind of Reckoning

> In order to establish the 'thousand-year Reich', the Germans set out to accomplish the extermination or permanent weakening of the racial and national groups of Europe or of those sections, such as the intelligentsia, on which the survival of these groups must largely depend. The converse to methods designed to decrease the birth-rate in occupied territories was the artificial increase in the birth-rate of Germans.
>
> *Sir Hartley Shawcross,*
> *British Attorney-General, at the main Nuremberg trial, July 1946*

War trials have nothing to do with justice: if they had, many more than twelve Nazis would have been sentenced to death at Nuremberg for the prosecution of a war in which millions died, some in battle and others as a result of a deliberate policy of extermination. Most acts of modern warfare, by any rational definition, can be construed as offences against humanity. Without question the worst of the German atrocities were infinitely more despicable than anything the Allies committed, but some actions of the Russians (the Katyn massacre), the British (the bombing of Dresden) and the Americans (Hiroshima) would properly have been regarded as war crimes if the other side had won.

If war is the continuation of politics by other means, then war trials are equally so. The postwar arraignment of important German soldiers and officials was in part about settling scores and bringing home to Germans the extent of their national shame. Yet they were conducted when the Western nations were already fearful of the threat posed by their erstwhile allies, the Soviet communists. The priority of the United States, France and Britain was to establish a strong West Germany as a bulwark against communism. Complicity in the Nazis' excesses had been so widespread among leading Germans that the process of reconstruction would take infinitely longer if everyone with the slightest taint were to be excluded from it.

Mindful of the consequences of the tough measures imposed on Germany after the First World War, which paved the way for the rise of Hitler, the victorious Western nations were cautious about being seen to be too harsh this time. That was why they eschewed the more ruthless approach of the Russians in the territories that the Red Army had liberated: there many leading SS men were executed, often in public and after the briefest of trials. Of the 35,000 German convictions for war crimes, by far the greater number were obtained in the East.

Much of the point of the Nuremberg trials as instruments of vengeance had been destroyed by the suicide as the war ended of some of the most important Nazi leaders. By choosing not to face the world's judgment, Hitler, Himmler and Goebbels pre-empted the court's decisions. And Göring escaped execution by killing himself after being sentenced to death.

Yet although in some respects the trials were a charade, their results were not a foregone conclusion. While all the defendants had been involved in the war effort at a senior level, the Allies recognised varying degrees of criminal responsibility. The trial of those involved in the Lebensborn movement has been criticised because at the end many of the Nazis' former opponents – and certainly the majority of their victims – thought the defendants had been let off too lightly, indeed virtually scot-free.

The Allies agreed as early as 1943, at a meeting of foreign ministers in Moscow, that, assuming they won the war, they would mount show trials of the German leaders. In August 1945 they decided to hold the trials in the historic German city of Nuremberg, beginning with the twenty-four surviving 'main war criminals', including Göring, Hess, von Ribbentrop, Speer and the missing Martin Bormann. They wanted a reasonably quick trial, believing that public interest would wane if it went on too long, and that this would defeat the principal object. In fact the trial lasted nearly a year, starting in November 1945 and ending on 1 October 1946. Twelve of the defendants were sentenced to death, three were acquitted and the rest imprisoned.

The trials of lesser officials were allowed to meander on for years, not ending until 1949. Case No. 8 at the American Military Tribunal No. 1, the so-called 'RuSHA case', dealt with the activities of the SS Race Office and the Lebensborn organisation. It lasted about eight months. Indictments were served at the beginning of July 1947 and the case came to court that October, with judgments handed down in March 1948. The indictment began thus:

> The United States of America, by the undersigned Telford Taylor, Chief of Counsel for War Crimes, duly appointed to represent said Government in the prosecution of war criminals, charges that the defendants herein committed crimes against humanity and war crimes . . . These crimes included murders, brutalities, cruelties, tortures, atrocities, deportation, enslavement, plunder of property, persecutions and other inhumane acts, as set forth in counts one and two of this indictment. All but one of the defendants herein are further charged with membership of a criminal organisation.

There were fourteen defendants, including Sollmann, Ebner and Inge Viermetz: the only woman in the dock, she was the only one not charged with belonging to the SS. The accused were drawn from four organisations, all sub-divisions of the SS: Lebensborn, RuSHA, the RKFDV (Office of the Reich Commissioner for Strengthening Germanism) and VoMi (Office for the Repatriation of Ethnic Germans), which had been responsible for kidnapping children in occupied territories. The prosecution said that their crimes against humanity and war crimes arose out of 'a systematic programme of genocide, aimed at the destruction of foreign nations and ethnic groups, in part by murderous extermination and in part by elimination and suppression of national characteristics'. The indictment went on:

> The object of the programme was to strengthen the German nation and the so-called Aryan race at the expense of other nations and groups by imposing Nazi and German characteristics upon individuals selected therefrom (such imposition hereinafter called Germanisation), and by the extermination of 'undesirable' racial elements.

The word 'genocide', meaning in essence the attempt to obliterate an entire race or to place it in subjection, was coined by Professor Raphael Lemkin of the War Department in Washington at the end of the war. It was recognised as a crime by the United Nations in 1946 and in 1948 the Genocide Convention was adopted by the UN General Assembly.

The indictment in the RuSHA case went on to list the methods allegedly used to carry out the defendants' objectives:

- Kidnapping the children of foreign nationals and selecting those considered of racial value for Germanisation;
- Compelling Eastern workers to have abortions both to preserve their working capacity and to weaken Eastern nations;
- Taking away children born to Eastern workers, for extermination or Germanisation;
- Executing or imprisoning Eastern workers who had sexual intercourse with Germans, and imprisoning the Germans involved;
- Hampering reproduction of enemy nationals;
- Evacuating enemy populations from their native lands and resettling ethnic Germans;
- Compelling foreign nationals to become German citizens and to join the German armed forces;
- Plundering public and private property and personal effects in Germany and the occupied territories;
- Participating in the persecution and extermination of Jews.

The role played by each of the four SS agencies in these activities was described in the indictment. When it came to Lebensborn, it noted:

Lebensborn was responsible, among other things, for the kidnapping of foreign children for the purpose of Germanisation. Max Sollmann was the chief of Lebensborn and in personal charge of Main Department A, which consisted of offices for reception into homes, guardianship, foster homes and adoption, statistics and registration; Gregor Ebner was the chief of the Main Health Department; Gunter Tesch was chief of the Main

Legal Department; and Inge Viermetz was the deputy chief of Main Department A.

There followed a concise description of the fundamental purpose of the operation: to proclaim and safeguard the supposed superiority of Nordic blood and to exterminate all sources that might dilute or taint it. The underlying objective was 'to assure Nazi dominance over Germany and German dominance over Europe in perpetuity'.

The indictment set out the detailed operation of the programme to kidnap foreign children, with its manifold motives: not just to weaken enemy nations but also to increase the population of Germany, and as an instrument of retaliation and intimidation in the occupied countries. Czech, Polish, Yugoslav and Norwegian children were the principal victims.

The general programme of Germanisation called for a special effort to be made to get racially valuable children who could be bred as a contribution to the greater German Reich. Moreover, children of foreign birth could be moulded and shaped into Nazis much more easily than their parents. Thus it came about that Lebensborn took over the kidnapping of so-called 'racially valuable' foreign children ... Also included in this programme were the illegitimate children of non-German mothers, fathered by members of the German armed forces in the occupied countries. Those children considered to be racially valuable were selected for Germanisation and placed in foster homes. In carrying out this programme, numerous birth certificates were falsified and German names were given to children selected for Germanisation.

Although Himmler was dead, his spirit hovered over the trial and the prosecution's opening statement contained several extracts from his speeches. 'We stand or die with this supreme blood of Germany,' he had said in February 1940, 'and if the good blood is not reproduced we will not be able to rule the world.'

Himmler's encouragement of illegitimate conception, especially when men were about to leave for the front, was also quoted. Evidence was given of his efforts in the occupied territories to ensure that local women made pregnant by German SS men or police should only be allowed to complete the pregnancy if the chance of a racially desirable baby was strong. In 1943 he issued a decree saying that abortions must be carried out on these women, by SS or police doctors, 'unless the woman is of good stock which must be ascertained in advance'. This served two purposes: keeping the race pure and allowing the woman to carry on working for the Reich. If the woman was of a high enough racial quality she would be sent to a Lebensborn home. After the birth the baby would be kept at the home for eventual adoption and the woman sent back to her country to resume working. If she later took German nationality and married a German, she could get her child back.

The prosecutors made much of the persecution and extermination of Jews and Eastern European peoples, describing them in some detail: the barbarism of Auschwitz and the Lidice massacre in Czechoslovakia were denounced at length. Himmler's apologia for the ruthless extermination of the Polish intelligentsia was quoted: 'They had to be done away with. There was no other way . . . The Poles got the shock they had to get.'

Then there was his speech to SS officers in Poznan in October 1943, in which he addressed the question of the brutal methods used to exterminate the Jews:

> It appalled everyone, and yet everyone was certain that he would do it next time if such orders were issued and if it were necessary . . . To have stuck it out and at the same time – apart from exceptions caused by human weakness – to have remained decent fellows, that is what has made us hard . . . We know how difficult we should have made it for ourselves if – with the bombing raids, the burdens and the deprivations of war – we still had Jews today in every town as secret saboteurs, agitators and troublemakers.

One reason for highlighting the Lidice massacre in the opening statement was that there was documentary evidence to link the Lebensborn organisation with the fate of the children whose parents were murdered there. With most of the Lebensborn files having been destroyed in 1945, such hard evidence was rare.

Himmler had written to Sollmann on 21 June, a few days after the atrocity, suggesting he go to Prague and discuss the children's fate with Karl Frank, the German administrator. Sollmann duly made the journey. There was also correspondence in 1944, concerning some of the Lidice children who were not among the thirteen originally chosen for Germanisation. They had been re-examined in their Czech detention camps and another seven were passed as racially sound and earmarked for Lebensborn homes, although their eventual fate is uncertain. The remainder were supposed to be sent as slave labour to other parts of the Reich, but the letter, from a colonel in Frank's office, said this could not be done without causing unrest among the populace, because many of their relatives had discovered where they were being held and were in contact with them. To move them might imperil 'the maintenance of industrial peace necessary for the unlimited production of war materials'.

The prosecution pointed out that 'there was not just one, but many Lidices in occupied Europe'. The smaller Czech village of Lezaky was razed just two weeks after Lidice: of its thirteen children, two were selected for Germanisation and adoption. Children were also kidnapped under similar conditions from the Ukraine, Poland, Yugoslavia and Romania. In June 1942 there was a punitive action against villages in Upper Carniola and Lower Styria in Yugoslavia, known to be centres of anti-Nazi partisan activity. Himmler demanded reports on the 'numbers and racial value of these children'. Later documents show that the children were sent to refugee camps where Inge Viermetz was among the officials who examined them. Those that fell into categories one and two – the most valuable blood – were sent to Lebensborn homes.

A report from Ebner to Sollmann on Romanian children was produced at the trial. He said that twenty-five of them had been taken into detention but only two were suitable for Germanisation. Most of the remainder were too old but three were so genetically inferior that they should be sterilised – a girl because 'the young men in the camp are getting interested in her', one boy because he might have tuberculosis and another boy because 'his skull looks mis-shapen, his ears stand out and his shoulders droop'.

The horrors of the punitive massacres and the concentration camps had been the subject of other Nuremberg trials. In bringing them into this one at this early stage, the prosecution was seeking to establish the intrinsic link between the twin aspects of the Nazis' racial policy

– the elimination of bad or impure blood and its replacement by good Nordic stock. 'First,' said the prosecutor, 'they wanted to strengthen the German people, both in numbers and in quality; second to weaken and eventually destroy national groups in the occupied countries.'

Logically this presentation of the case, putting the race-enhancing measures into the context of the Nazis' broader aims, cannot be faulted. In tactical terms the prosecution might have been better advised to play down the more lurid crimes in this particular trial. Although RuSHA and its agencies were clearly involved in the total strategy that lay behind the brutality, it was impossible to pin specific blame for the murders on any of the defendants in this case. The prosecution drew attention to operational links between the two aspects of the programme, such as the fact that some Lebensborn homes were equipped with stolen Jewish furniture; but compared with the acts of mass murder that had been described to the court, these seemed minor offences, equivalent to being an accessory after the fact.

While it is clear that kidnapping children and racial manipulation are evil, they are palpably less horrendous crimes than those that took place in the concentration camps and can be made to look comparatively insignificant if the two classes of offences are considered together. This may, in the end, have been a factor in persuading the court to deal with the Lebensborn defendants leniently.

The most affecting witnesses at the trial were the stolen children themselves. Now teenagers, they had unwittingly found themselves victims of the Nazis' preposterous attempts to wipe out their past and reinvent them as good citizens of the Reich. Most of them appeared for the prosecution but a few supported the case for the defence.

One of the prosecution witnesses was Slavonmir Paczesny, a Polish boy of fifteen who had been ten when removed from his home in Lodz by the Brown Sisters in 1942. He was taken to the children's home in the city and photographed from the standard three angles. His father had tried to get him back from the home but had been turned away. His mother came to visit him but she too was not allowed inside and they could talk only through the wire fence. Then, along with about thirty other children, he was taken to the home at Kalisz. Here is an extract from his testimony:

'Were you taught to speak and read German at Kalisz?'

'Yes.'

'Were you Polish children allowed to speak Polish among yourselves?'

'We were not allowed to do it but I did it secretly.'

'If any of the children spoke Polish, what happened? Were they punished?'

'Yes.'

'Were you ever punished?'

'Yes, I was.'

'What did they do to you?'

'They shut me up in a room and gave me neither dinner nor supper.'

'Did your mother ever come and see you while you were in Kalisz?'

'Yes, my mother came.'

'Did you get to speak with your mother at Kalisz?'

'No, I did not.'

'How did you know that she came?'

'Other children saw her.'

From Kalisz the children were sent to Salzburg, where they were given new names and told to forget all about Poland because they would not be going back. They were not allowed to write or receive letters from their families but occasionally they managed to evade the restrictions. Slavonmir was renamed Karl Grohmann and was soon adopted by a farming family. After four months, though, he was taken away from the farm because he had made contact with Polish-speaking Serbian soldiers stationed nearby. He was moved to a second farm where he was found by Polish troops after the war and returned home.

Another who appeared for the prosecution was Maria Hanfova, from Lidice, who had been twelve years old on that fateful night when the Germans came to destroy the Czech village. She told of being woken at 3 a.m., being taken with her mother to a nearby school and, two days later, watching her mother being loaded with the other women into a truck. Then Maria and the other children were put on the train for Lodz.

'On your way to Lodz, how were you treated?'
'Very badly.'
'Would you describe what you mean by bad treatment?'
'We were given little to eat – just black coffee and bread –
and the children were hungry. They cried and asked for their
mothers.'
'Were there nurses on the train to take care of the young
children?'
'There were nurses with us and they took care of the little
children, but very badly.'

At Lodz, Maria was one of the seven Lidice children chosen as
being of pure enough race for adoption by German parents. They
were, she said, also treated badly at the camp and were forbidden
to ask questions about the fate of their parents or their friends who
had failed the selection process. Then they were moved to the home at
Puschkau where they were taught German and punished if they were
caught speaking Czech. They were never told what had happened
to their parents and, like the Polish children, were not allowed to
write letters.

'What did they say when you told them, if you ever did, that
you wanted to go back home?'
'I was always told that we were not to go back but we were
to stay in Germany.'

At Puschkau her name was changed to Maria Hanff. After a year
there she was sent to the Richter family in Dessau and her name
changed again – to Marga Richter. There too, she said, she had been
treated badly by the family:

'Did they ever say anything about you being a Czech?'
'Yes, they did.'
'What did they say?'
'That I am from Czechoslovakia and now I have to listen

to the Germans, that I will become a German; that I have to be against the Czechs ... I was also given a German Hitler Youth uniform.'

The prosecution's purpose in drawing from the children such details of their treatment was to contest the assertion by the defendants – in effect their plea of mitigation – that the children had been well cared for. Anticipating this line of defence, and the claim that Lebensborn was essentially a compassionate organisation, kind to the children in its care, the prosecutor had said in his opening statement:

Many times throughout this proceeding we shall hear the defendants say how well the children were treated and speak of the wonderful care afforded them. In comparison to the treatment of other children whom these defendants rejected for Germanization this may well be true. But it is no defence for a kidnapper to say that he treated his victim well. Even more important, we must ask ourselves why they were so treated. The answer is simple – these innocent children were abducted for the very purpose of being indoctrinated with Nazi ideology and brought up as 'good' Germans. This serves to aggravate, not mitigate the crime.

While the logic of that is irrefutable, one effect of pursuing that line in questioning the children was to obscure the principal ways in which they had been 'treated badly': that they had been forcibly removed from their parents, who had been murdered or sent to concentration camps, and then the children had been forced to change their national identity. Those were the real crimes, and there was no dispute that they had happened. What the defendants and their lawyers contested was the number of children involved and the Lebensborn organisation's degree of complicity.

One of the defence witnesses was Lucie Bergner, sixteen at the time of the trial. She was brought on to the stand to support the contention of the defendants that most of the Polish children were taken from their homes as a social service, for their own good. Lucie had no

recollection of her natural parents and had been living with her sick
and elderly grandmother near Poznan when the Germans took her
away to a children's home. Her grandmother, who spoke German
as well as Polish, had always told her that her parents had wanted
her to be fostered. Because of the old woman's increasing frailty, she
had wanted to be rid of the girl for some time and was therefore glad
when the Germans came to take Lucie away.

The girl was sent initially to Kaliscz, but her account of conditions was markedly different from that of the other children
sent there.

> 'The children among themselves, what language did they
> speak?'
> 'They spoke Polish.'
> 'Did the governesses like that, or didn't they?'
> 'Oh yes, they liked it.'
> 'Did they object to it or prohibit it?'
> 'Oh no, never.'
> 'Remember very clearly, or try to remember as clearly as
> you can, whether there was a case when punishment was
> administered for that reason.'
> 'No, I can't remember any.'

After Kaliscz she was sent to the Oberweiss home in Austria. Again
her memory of conditions there was in conflict with that of many
former inmates:

> 'And how did they treat you at Oberweiss?'
> 'I liked it so much.'
> 'Tell me why you liked it so much. You seem to remember
> it very fondly.'
> 'We got everything and we could do as we pleased. We got
> good food.'
> 'Were you punished in any way at Oberweiss?'
> 'No . . . they didn't punish us at all.'
> 'Do you know anything about the fact that children were

supposed to have been locked in a cellar underneath the earth, which was dark?'

'Oh no, there wasn't even a cellar at Oberweiss.'

From Oberweiss, Lucie was taken away by foster parents, the Treibers, where again she fell on her feet, and was 'kept as if I was their own daughter'. The defence counsel asked:

> 'Will you please tell me now quite frankly how you like staying with your foster parents?'
> 'I like it there very much . . .'
> 'Would you ever like to leave again?'
> 'No, I would not.'

It would have been surprising if there were not some children glad to be getting out of Poland, where wartime life was hard, and some people who had been looking after them in the absence of their parents must equally have been relaxed about letting them go. However, Lucie Bergner's evidence contradicts the stories we heard of weeping mothers watching as their children were taken away on trains, and trying desperately to see them at the camps where they were initially taken. Yet the defence lawyers had done well to find a handful of children, in a similar position to Lucie, who had integrated well into their new German families and were reluctant to be uprooted again. They enabled the accused to mount a strong defence against the charge of kidnapping foreign children and forcibly removing them. Sollmann's counsel said, with perhaps a hint of irony:

> To be sure, the prosecution emphasises in its indictment that the crime of kidnapping is in many ways worse than any other crime, as perhaps the mass murder of the Jews, the atrocities of the concentration camps, the inhuman medical experiments, etc. But the prosecution has not said what it understands by the crime of kidnapping, what the characteristics of a crime of this sort are.

The defence counsel said how despicable it would be to take a child away from its parents and move it by force to a foreign country; how that could have the effect of weakening the ethnic make-up of the child's country of origin. His point was that the prosecution had failed to establish that the defendants were responsible for any such crimes:

> We are not dealing with the moral evaluation of abstract facts but rather with the deeds of Max Sollmann and his co-workers. These deeds have as little connection with such a criminal act or with any other punishable offence as the proper acts of a doctor have with bodily injury or some such offence.

In other words, even if those crimes had taken place they were not the responsibility of the accused who had, by contrast, acted to alleviate suffering rather than inflict it. Making the claim that before the occupation the Poles had systematically placed ethnic German children in orphanages, and destroyed all evidence of their parentage, the defence lawyer argued that racial screening of such children was necessary, for their own good, to determine their origin and decide whether to have them fostered or adopted by German families.

The defence relied heavily on the argument that by far the greatest number of the children taken from Poland were ethnic German orphans and to support their case they quoted the 1941 order by General Ulrich Greifelt, head of the SS in Poland and the senior defendant at the trial. However, as the prosecution pointed out, this order stated that children should be taken not only if their 'racial appearance leads to the assumption of Nordic parentage', but also if they were 'recognized as bearers of blood valuable to Germany'. Greifelt decreed that suitable children should be placed in the care of childless SS families.

The defence counsel countered by arguing that, whatever the grounds for selection, the Lebensborn organisation had nothing to do with the children until they had already been taken from their homes by other authorities. He insisted that the racial tests were not designed to 'separate the loot according to wheat and chaff' but, in the absence of any records of the children's origin, to gain evidence to help the authorities decide if they really were ethnic Germans.

To say that the Government of the Third Reich did not, after the occupation of Poland, turn its attention first to orphans of ethnic origin in Polish orphanages, but had by force taken children without regard to this, children that were of Polish origin but had a Germanic appearance ... would be to fundamentally misunderstand the leading circles of the Third Reich and to accuse them of betraying their own ideology of blood and race.

Explaining what he meant by that, the defence lawyer said that it was not just a Nazi concept that a large and strong country would seek to keep to a minimum 'the number of those who want to participate in the honour and advantages that accrue to such a strong nation'. Nearly all countries exercised a measure of control over who could and who could not claim citizenship. For that reason, it was illusory to believe that the Germans would have wanted to abduct foreign children and turn them into Nazis.

Because the defendants maintained that most of the children were originally German anyway, the lawyer used the term 're-Germanisation' to describe the process of educating them in the language and culture of their new homeland. He said that the Lebensborn personnel played no part in this procedure and had no more knowledge of it than the average citizen – despite evidence from some of the children that racial examinations and other tests had taken place at Lebensborn homes:

The fact that the staff of the Lebensborn used terms like 'suitable for Germanisation', etc., proves at most the vague notion prevailing in the Lebensborn in respect of these ideas ... Moreover, in respect of selection and instruction of the foster parents the Lebensborn has shown a complete lack of political interest. It is by no means true that the children were placed predominantly in the homes of SS families ... The sole aim was that the children were cared for with love and grew up under the best possible conditions ... The defendant Max Sollmann and the other members of the Lebensborn staff felt before their conscience a personal responsibility that these valuable goods which they were to care for should not be harmed.

This was the whole tone of the defence: that the taking of the children was not criminal, because they were Germans who should by rights be in Germany; and that even if a crime had been committed it was not by Lebensborn personnel, who were concerned only for the well-being of the precious human cargo in their charge. Counsel went on:

> If towards these allegedly abducted children the intentions had been of the kind imputed by the prosecution, they certainly would not have been brought into these well-to-do families but into institutions fashioned after the model of the Prussian military orphanages, perhaps with a National Socialist variation. The foster parents loved and cared for these children as though they had been their own and the Lebensborn, when it demanded educational reports, was only interested to know if the children were well off physically and mentally, not whether they were properly 'Germanised' or had become good National Socialists.

The prosecution contested most of these claims, adding that even if the Germanised children had been considerately looked after – at least compared with those who failed the racial tests – this did nothing to mitigate the crime of kidnapping. With respect to the claim that most of the children were anyway ethnic Germans, prosecuting counsel quoted Himmler's instructions that 'racially good types' be Germanised whatever their origins:

> The documents leave no doubt that the defendants, the leading members of RuSHA, knew that in executing Greifelt's order they had to deal with children who not only were foreign nationals but belonged to non-German ethnic groups as well. Several documents originating in RuSHA speak of 'Germanising orphans of foreign blood', 'Germanisation of names of foreign orphans' and 'orphans of aliens'. It is significant that in the statements of RuSHA concerning racial qualities of children there are no statements to the effect that the examination of these children proved them to be of German blood . . . [but] speak of them only as of 'desirable increase of population'.

As for those kidnapped children who had told the court that they wanted to stay in Germany, the prosecution responded:

Their testimony shows that they were seized at such an early age that few even remember their parents or relatives. The greater portion of the lives of these young witnesses has been spent with the German foster parents with whom they were placed by Lebensborn and thus it is only natural that the children have developed a false sense of security during these early years of their lives . . . That the decision of these immature children to remain in Germany should be decisive is absurd.

Greifelt, in his closing statement, defended his actions:

I felt myself to be a servant of these people who were uprooted from their previous homes. I devoted myself to the foundation of a new life for them, to the consolidation of their existence and thereby of their Germanism. That was my task. At no time did I even have a spark of an idea to do harm to other human beings on account of them, to torture or destroy them . . . I do not feel guilty.

Ebner did not feel guilty either:

When I went to Lebensborn, I was prompted by my devotion to the medical profession and my compassion for mothers and children who, because of wrong moral conceptions, were not or could not be cared for by their own people and were covered with shame . . . I have within me the inner peace of the philosopher.

Sollmann said he had welcomed the chance to refute 'the inconceivable assertions of the prosecution, assertions which will for all time remain incomprehensible to me'. And the defence lawyers continued to maintain that the accused were engaged in a 'work of mercy':

It is quite certain that the Lebensborn was never involved in any criminal programme. It set out upon its course guided by the most humane and natural idea which one can imagine and remained true to this idea, which constituted its highest law and programme, as long as it existed – the idea of chivalrous protection for the expectant mother and loving care for her child.

The court dealt leniently with the defendants from the Lebensborn organisation, but less so with those who had been associated with RuSHA and the SS command structure – including Greifelt – who received terms of imprisonment ranging from life to ten years. Although all the Lebensborn defendants except Inge Viermetz were found guilty of belonging to a criminal organisation (the SS), they were cleared on the substantive counts of the indictment and were released at the end of the trial on 10 March 1948, the tribunal taking into account that they had already spent nearly three years in detention. Lee Wyatt, the presiding judge, explained the decision thus:

> It is quite clear from the evidence that the Lebensborn Society, which existed long prior to the war, was a welfare institution and primarily a maternity home. From the beginning, it cared for mothers, both married and unmarried, and children, both legitimate and illegitimate. The prosecution has failed to prove with requisite certainty the participation of Lebensborn, and the defendants connected therewith, in the kidnapping programme conducted by the Nazis. While the evidence has disclosed that thousands and thousands of children were unquestionably kidnapped by other agencies or organisations and brought into Germany, the evidence has also disclosed that only a small percentage of the total number ever found their way into Lebensborn. And of this number only in isolated instances did Lebensborn take children who had a living parent. The majority of these children in any way connected with Lebensborn were orphans of ethnic Germans . . . When it was discovered that the child had a living parent, Lebensborn did not proceed with adoption, as in the case of orphans, but simply allowed the child to be placed in a German home after investigation of the German family.

So the judge reached this somewhat surprising conclusion:

> It is quite clear from the evidence that of the numerous organisations operating in Germany who were connected with

foreign children brought into Germany, Lebensborn was the one organisation which did everything in its power to adequately provide for the children and protect the legal interests of the children placed in its care.

One of the three judges, Daniel O'Connell, delivered a dissenting opinion – though not, as some of the victims may have wished, on the grounds that the tribunal had been too lenient, but that some of the sentences on the SS defendants, including Greifelt, had been too harsh. 'Severity of sentence is erroneously believed by many to be a preventive of future crime by others. I do not subscribe to such a belief.'

Judge O'Connell said that the men, although they enjoyed military rank, had been engaged in essentially civilian tasks:

All governments engaging in war, of necessity, must have the aid of civilian bureaus operating under governmental direction, and functioning closely with the armed forces. It is difficult to draw a line fixing to what extent punishment can be inflicted upon those associated with civilian bureaus ... It is also most difficult to determine to what extent the civilian bureau official joins in spirit, or without definite objection or protest, against acts calculated to further the perpetration of criminal acts.

The result of the trial caused scarcely a ripple in a world which, three years after the war, was keen to move forward rather than look back. In London, *The Times* reported it in a single paragraph, concentrating entirely on the jail sentences meted out to the SS principals. Headlined 'Himmler's Associates Sentenced', it read in full:

Eight heavy sentences of imprisonment were passed by an American military tribunal at Nuremberg on the leaders of Himmler's Race and Settlement Office who have been on trial for several months on charges bearing on the new crime of 'genocide'. Ulrich Greifelt, the main defendant, received sentence of life imprisonment and the seven other sentences ranged from 25 years to 10 years. Inge Viermetz, the only woman in the case, was acquitted.

The report did not mention that the Lebensborn officials had received the lightest of sentences. There was little general interest in the organization but, among those who knew it, many were offended by the leniency of the verdict on the Lebensborn officials. Among them were such as Roman Hrabar, who was still trying to trace Polish and other children who had been absorbed into the German populace. It was clear to him that, with the Cold War in place, he could expect minimal help from Western governments in taking kidnapped children back east; but he would have liked to have seen the crimes acknowledged as crimes.

In February 1950, responding to pressure and as part of their continuing (though some claimed less than wholehearted) attempt to purge the Nazi past, the German authorities themselves staged a trial of Ebner, Sollmann and several of their senior aides. The trial took place in Munich and lasted six working days. The prosecution sought to refute Sollmann's assertion at Nuremberg – accepted by Judge Wyatt – that Lebensborn had been a benign organisation, innocent of complicity in the attempt to destroy the Polish or any other nation. Quoting Himmler's 1943 speech about 'robbing and stealing' good blood, the indictment stated:

> As leader of Lebensborn, Max Sollmann had knowledge of the Germanisation programme ... As a member of the personal staff of the *Reichsführer SS*, he had without doubt knowledge of the internal affairs of the SS.

He must, therefore, have been aware of the full implication of Greifelt's order of February 1942 about the Germanisation of Polish children. The prosecution produced statements from Polish children and others to refute the claims of Lebensborn personnel that they were working in good faith and treated the children well. A woman who had worked as a typist at the Munich headquarters stated that 'the majority of children coming from Poland did not look upon their Germanisation positively', as was shown by their always speaking Polish among themselves, and their attempts to write letters to Poland, even though it was against the rules. From this the prosecution inferred:

> Thus it is clear that the Lebensborn leadership were fully aware of what was going on and did not act in good faith; this was

to do with foreign children who were forced to change their national identity ... It is not too difficult to envisage how the children were separated from their mothers.

The indictment then described in detail how, in defiance of German law, the registration documents of the stolen children had been altered to hide their true origins. Their place of birth was normally given as Posen (Poznan), their ages assessed by Ebner and their names changed to those of their new families. Sollmann, Ebner and their senior colleagues 'all worked together against the law ... They were aware of how children were taken away from their parents and they conspired in a programme of stealing children'.

Inge Viermetz, who was cleared of all charges at Nuremberg, was singled out in the Munich indictment as having had special responsibility for the acceptance of foreign children into Lebensborn homes and for establishing new homes in occupied territories. Ebner, as the head doctor, had primary responsibility for racial checking and also, with Sollmann, played a role in taking Jewish property for the homes and employing concentration camp inmates as slave labour, working from 6 a.m. to 7 p.m. daily.

Sollmann and Ebner repeated their Nuremberg defence that the Lebensborn homes were primarily a benign social service and that racial selection was an insignificant aspect of their work. They said that they never received direct instructions from the SS. Sollmann explained that after 1940 only half the births in the homes were illegitimate, whereas before the figure had been 80 per cent. The average birthrate in the homes over their nine-year existence was about 100 babies a month. Sollmann added that he had been personally opposed to extending the Lebensborn homes to countries outside Germany and had always been reluctant to take in foreign children, although he admitted his role in receiving the selected children from the destroyed Czech village of Lidice: given that the documents about this had survived, there was no point in his denying it.

Several witnesses spoke up in favour of Sollmann, including people who had worked at Lebensborn headquarters. The court was told that he stuck less rigidly to the official racial criteria for mothers than had his predecessor Pflaum; that he allowed Polish children contact with their relatives if they sought it and that he was quite lenient to the workers from concentration camps – not housing them behind barbed wire as he was supposed to do and even putting on film shows for them. One former prisoner said it was regarded as a privilege to work at a Lebensborn home, and there was evidence given that Sollmann had disciplined an employee for striking a Dutch prisoner.

However, the impression that all was sweetness and light at the homes was punctured somewhat by the evidence of Dr Brandenburg, an air force medical officer transferred to the Lebensborn organisation in the spring of 1944 and later that year sent to the home at Wernigerode in central Germany. There, he maintained, a sister named Luise Wimmer made advances to him and when he rejected them she furiously reported him to Ebner for spreading alarm and despondency among the inmates. (Wimmer admitted reporting Brandenburg, but told the court that it was he who had made advances towards her.) An opponent of Nazi philosophy, the doctor had apparently been telling the mothers – accurately, as it turned out – that the Russians were moving in for the kill and that the German skies were dominated by British and American aircraft.

Ebner told the court that he reported the matter to Sollmann and demanded that Brandenburg be moved from the home. Brandenburg said Ebner told him he would report the matter personally to Himmler and that he would ensure he was never able to practise medicine again. He did leave the home and later that year faced an SS tribunal in Berlin, accused of spreading hostile propaganda. The SS judge, joking that he would have been better advised to have responded to the sister's advances in the first place, stripped him of his rank and he ended the war in prison.

At the end of the Munich trial the public prosecutor asked that Sollmann and Ebner be sentenced respectively to two and four years in a work camp and be made to give up half their future earnings. In fact the tribunal was much more lenient. Sollmann was sentenced to thirty days' special work, the loss of 30 per cent of his earnings and the loss of his rights to own a car, vote or take any active part in politics. For five years he was not allowed to work as a teacher, preacher, writer or broadcaster. Ebner received sixty days' special work and the loss of half his earnings, as well as the other restrictions imposed on Sollmann. The remaining six defendants were not punished.

The court explained why Ebner had been treated more harshly than Sollmann. Before and during the war Ebner had been an active Nazi propagandist, giving lectures on racial and other matters. 'The accused remained a convinced National Socialist until 1945.' The court also took into account his apparent role in denouncing the luckless Dr Brandenburg to the SS. 'On the whole attitude of the accused, the court must conclude that he has not taken an upright stance in these matters and has tried to cover up certain facts.'

Sollmann, on the other hand, had made a more favourable impression. He seemed to have protected some people who fell foul of the regime and the court took account of evidence that he ensured that prisoners working at the homes were treated well. 'He might be defined as one who refused the brutal measures of the regime and in at least this way showed themselves to be opponents of the regime.'

The trial at Munich was the last formal attempt by postwar Germany to exorcise the Lebensborn idea. Although in terms of punishment the court had been scarcely harsher to the Lebensborn leaders than had the American tribunal at Nuremberg, at least the Munich judge recognised that grave crimes had been committed in the homes, and that the people in charge must accept responsibility. After that, the book was officially closed on the most spectacularly misconceived racial experiment in history.

10

Born-Again Eugenics

The idea of 'race purity' may have died; the idea of building a strain of supermen may have died; but the idea that it is more beneficial for certain people to have children than others, and that a vast range of human problems can be cured once we learn how to manipulate our genes, remains very much with us.

Ruth Hubbard, and Elijah Wald
in Exploding the Gene Myth, 1993

It was only to be expected that the science of eugenics should forfeit credibility and respect after being so misused and corrupted by Hitler, Himmler and their fellow zealots. The word itself became tainted by the uses it had been put to. In *The Nazi Connection*, Stefan Kühl wrote in 1994:

The pride with which scientists in the 1910s, 1920s and 1930s referred to themselves as eugenicists had evaporated. After World War Two, eugenicists described themselves as 'population scientists', 'human geneticists', 'psychiatrists', 'sociologists', 'anthropologists' and 'family politicians' in an attempt to avoid eugenics terminology.

Learned journals were renamed. The *Annals of Eugenics* became the *Annals of Human Genetics* and *Eugenics Quarterly* was transformed into the *Journal of Social Biology*. *Eugenics Review* closed in 1984 and is now incorporated in the *Journal of Biosocial Science*. In America the Eugenics Records Office changed its name to the Cold Spring Harbor Laboratory. London also had a Eugenics Record Office, founded by Sir Francis Galton in 1904: it became the

Francis Galton Laboratory for National Eugenics not long after its foundation but is now known simply as the Galton Laboratory. The Eugenics Society, founded in 1907, is now the Galton Institute. It no longer espouses its original aim of eradicating 'the family stock which produces paupers, the feeble-minded, alcoholics and certain types of criminals'.

Although Galton was the founder of eugenics he is not held responsible by modern academics for its later misuse. His reputation among them remains high and his legacy is honoured at an annual symposium at the Galton Institute. The Galton Laboratory is part of the Department of Human Genetics and Biometry at University College, London – formerly called the Department of Eugenics, Biometry and Genetics. Since 1990 the Laboratory and the Department have been headed by Professor Steve Jones. In his 1994 book *The Language of the Genes* he wrote:

> The adulteration of human genetics reached its disastrous end in the Nazi experiment, and for many years it was seen as at best unfashionable to discuss the nature of inherited differences among people.

After fifty years that reluctance is waning. The subject is now being broached again, in no less controversial ways.

In Germany itself, some of the people and institutions involved in the scientific justification for genocide were able to carry on with their work after the war, with only minor shifts of focus to account for the new international climate. Kühl points out that as early as 1948 some psychiatrists who had been closely connected to the Nazis' elimination of handicapped people were reintegrated into the international scientific community and were able to participate in congresses, thanks in part to the support of American colleagues.

Among these was Dr Robert Ritter, the psychologist appointed in 1936 as Director of the Racial Hygiene and Hereditary Research Centre in the Reich Health Department. He had come to the attention of the Nazi authorities through his researches at the University of Tübingen into hereditary delinquency and feeble-mindedness, with special emphasis on gypsies, who offended established society in several European countries by their failure to conform to conventional norms. At the Health Department Ritter took on the task of categorising the 30,000 Sinti and Roma gypsies in Germany into groups based on racial purity. This done, they were forcibly rounded up and put into self-contained colonies. Himmler issued a decree in December 1938 ordering 'the physical separation of Gypsydom from the German nation, the prevention of miscegenation and finally the regulation of the way of life of pure and part-Gypsies'.

As Michael Burleigh and Wolfgang Wippermann record in *The Racial State*, official persecution of the gypsies continued in West Germany after the war, using records inherited from Ritter's department, and some members of Ritter's former staff retained their involvement in the process. In Switzerland, Ritter's theories were used for the same purpose. During the war, Ritter was appointed Director of the Criminal-Biological Institute of the German Security Police, where he looked at the hereditary aspects of juvenile delinquency. He was allowed to continue working as a child psychologist after the war.

The notorious Kaiser Wilhelm Institute, the centre of Nazi eugenic researches, remained in being after the war under Hans Nachstheim. He had played no direct role in any genocide but his friend Freiherr von Verschuer, who helped analyse Josef Mengele's experiments on dead Auschwitz prisoners, was soon back in the scientific mainstream. Despite being denounced by a de-Nazification tribunal as a fellow-traveller, Verschuer was appointed Professor of Human Genetics at Munster in 1951 and later became President of the German Society for Anthropology. Kühl wrote:

> Verschuer's case was all too typical. Other racial hygienists who played prominent roles in Nazi Germany quickly regained influential positions. Between 1946 and 1955, for example, Fritz Lenz, Günther Just and Heinrich Schade returned to professorships in German universities in human genetics, anthropology or psychiatry, not in racial hygiene or eugenics.

After his rehabilitation, Verschuer joined the editorial board of *The Mankind Quarterly*, which has provided an influential platform for modern proponents of eugenic and racial theories: he is therefore an important link between today's genetic controversies and the excesses of the Nazi past. A significant source of funding for the journal was the Pioneer Fund. This was founded in 1937 by Wickliffe Draper, a textile magnate, for the purpose of fostering research into 'race betterment with special reference to the people of the United States', specifically encouraging the propagation of descendants or relatives of 'white persons who settled in the original thirteen colonies prior to the adoption of the constitution'.

Draper was not deterred by the failure of the Nazis' racial programme in Germany and the Fund continued to give money for research in these fields after the war. Kühl writes:

> Today, the Pioneer Fund is the most important financial supporter of research concerning the connection between race and heredity in the United States. It also continues to finance studies in the areas of eugenics, human genetics and immigration.

In 1978 the *The Mankind Quarterly* appointed Roger Pearson as its editor. Pearson today heads the Institute for the Study of Man at McLean in Virginia, which has also received money from the Pioneer Fund. In the 1950s he helped found the Northern League, devoted to the 'interests and solidarity of all Teutonic nations'. The author in 1991 of *Race, Intelligence and Bias in Academe*, Pearson is one of the many controversial academics on the list of those who have received support over the years from the Fund – a list which, according to Kühl, 'reads partly like a *Who's Who* of scientific and political racism in the United States, Canada, Great Britain and Ireland'.

Two prominent recipients of Pioneer Fund grants were William Shockley and Arthur Jensen, who wrote books justifying their belief that intelligence was inherited and had little to do with environmental factors. They also held that black people were inherently less intelligent than white. Shockley, who won the Nobel Prize for Physics in 1956 for his invention of the transistor, suggested in 1970 that, to prevent the birth of large numbers of people of limited intelligence, low-IQ men and women should be paid for agreeing to be sterilised. The rate should be set at $1,000 for each IQ point below 100. Thus a 70-IQ moron capable of fathering perhaps twenty children should be paid $30,000. Shockley argued that each of these payments might save taxpayers as much as $250,000 through not having to care for the mentally retarded offspring of the man's liaisons.

The link between birth control and eugenics has always been strong. Marie Stopes, the pioneer of birth control in Britain, was an enthusiastic eugenicist, her proselytising efforts mostly directed at lowering the birth rate among the labouring poor in London's East End. Critics of internationally supported contraception programmes point out that it is always the developing countries and the poorest sections of society which are targeted. Advocates of birth control say this is because the poorest people invariably have the largest number of children. Their opponents say that it is a surreptitious way of achieving the Nazis' racial aims of suppressing those elements of society of which the ruling class does not approve.

The controversy over the inheritability of intelligence, the 'nature or nurture' debate, has raged throughout the second half of the twentieth century. The theory that intelligence, as measured by IQ tests, is transmitted through the genes, rather than absorbed through environment and education, is obviously helpful to those who believe in the concept of superior and inferior races.

It is hard to deny that inheritance plays a role in determining intelligence, but the controversy centres on just how large a role that is and whether race has any relevance to it. The fact that both race and mental capacity are to some extent inherited does not necessarily imply a correlation between the two. Some of the early evidence on inherited intelligence derived from the researches of Sir Cyril Burt on identical twins brought up in different environments, who tended to show similar results in IQ tests. Not long after Burt died in 1971 there were suggestions that some of his results had been falsified, but the extent and significance of his departure from rigorous scientific method is still in dispute.

Burt met Galton when he was a boy: he was the son of a doctor and Galton was one of his father's patients. Galton was one of the first scientists to suggest using identical twins for analysing the importance of heredity, and was also an early enthusiast for intelligence testing. In later years, according to his biographer L. S. Hearnshaw, Burt said that Galton was a major influence and inspiration to him.

The question of inherited intelligence, and its implicit racial overtones, became an issue on American and British college campuses in the late sixties and early seventies, the heyday of radical student protest. Scholars such as Jensen, Shockley, H. J. Eysenck and Richard Herrnstein, who were regarded as taking the 'nature' side in the nature versus nurture debate, received hostile receptions when they visited universities to give lectures, and sometimes were forced to cancel their appearances. They were abused as 'racists' and 'Fascists' because their work was interpreted as implying that some racial groups were inferior and would always remain so despite attempts to correct the balance through education or positive discrimination.

Herrnstein described his persecution by students in the appendix to his 1973 book *IQ in the Meritocracy*. The book was an expansion of an article in *Atlantic Monthly* two years earlier which had provoked the outcry against him. It argued that social mobility and promotion through merit would have the long-term effect of increasing the biological gap between social classes by enriching the intellectual capacity of the higher class at the expense of the lower:

> When people can freely take their natural level in society, the upper classes will, virtually by definition, have greater capacity than the lower ... The biological stratification of society looms.

He advocated intelligence and other testing to aid in the search for 'effective compensatory education' but added:

> Unfortunately, the odds are against that worthy cause as long as the egalitarian orthodoxy can portray the quest for understanding as apostasy ... The false belief in human equality leads to rigid, inflexible expectations, often doomed to frustration, thence to anger. Ever more shrilly, we call on our educational and social institutions to make everyone the same, when we should instead be trying to mould our institutions around the inescapable limitations and variations of human ability.

All this may seem some distance from the fanatical excesses of the Nazis; but in the political climate of the time it appeared to be based on the same fundamental principle, so it was reviled by the Left. Nature versus nurture has always been to a large extent a Right/Left split.

Twenty years later Herrnstein was involved in a comparable controversy, albeit posthumously. With Professor Charles Murray, a sociologist popular with right-wing thinkers, he wrote a book called *The Bell Curve*, but died just before it was published. This book addressed the racial issue much more directly than he had done in *IQ and the Meritocracy*. Its central argument was that black people are inherently less intelligent than whites – one figure quoted was that 6 per cent of blacks have an IQ of below 70, compared with 2 per cent of whites. Blacks, however, produce children at a faster rate – in part because white middle-class women with good jobs delay starting a family until quite late and thus have fewer children. As a result, the authors postulated that the average intelligence in the United States was on a long-term downward spiral. This was a very clear throwback to the views of the nineteenth-century eugenicists, so admired by Hitler, who deplored 'miscegenation' (a word coined in the United States in 1864) because it would water down the intellectual quality of the Aryan race.

The Bell Curve drew on the work of a number of academics in this field with controversial reputations, among them Richard Lynn, Professor of Psychology at the University of Ulster, a former member of the editorial board of *The Mankind Quarterly* and another beneficiary of a Pioneer Fund grant. Interviewed by Alasdair Palmer of *The Spectator* in February 1995, Lynn said:

> I am not a Nazi. There is nothing at all in accepting that the races are different in their intelligence potential that commits you to any particular social policy, still less to anything that resembles the crimes of the Nazis . . . You cannot refute a theory by pointing to the fact that unpleasant people have believed versions of it.

Lynn told Palmer that he had done less work on the question of inherited intelligence than J. Philippe Rushton, Professor of Psychology at the University of Western Ontario and author of *Race, Evolution and Behaviour*. Rushton is another leading toiler in this overworked field and yet another whose efforts are supported by the Pioneer Fund. His theory of racial difference varies in an important respect from that espoused by the Nazis. He divides mankind into three races: Negroids, Caucasoids and Mongoloids. The Negroids, or blacks, have the lowest intelligence potential but the Caucasoids, the whites, do not have the highest: that honour is reserved for the Mongoloids from eastern Asia, whose capabilities, according to Rushton's researches, exceed those of the white race. Hitler and Himmler would not have liked that.

Rushton's work has some peculiar ramifications. He places great store by the difference in penis size between races. 'It's a trade-off,' he has been quoted as saying. 'More brain or more penis. You can't have everything.' His somewhat haphazard researches convince him that black men have the largest penises and Asians the smallest. This finding links in with the fear, which he shares with the authors of *The Bell Curve*, of excessive reproduction by the less brainy races, so that in time they will overwhelm the less fertile but higher-achieving members of society.

Though widely reported and discussed (Lynn, for instance, has written on the features page of *The Times* of London) it is important to stress that these bizarre views are held by only a minority of scientists. When they publish findings of this nature they are invariably attacked by scholars with more mainstream views. At the 1995 meeting of the American Association for the Advancement of Science, Solomon Katz, Professor of Anthropology at the University of Pennsylvania, said:

> Nineteenth and early twentieth century categories of race, which today are thought to have little scientific merit, have often been used to support racist doctrines. Yet the concept persists as a social convention that fosters institutional discrimination ... It is outrageous to base judgments on research and findings that are clearly outdated. There is just no valid reason for using existing racial terms. This isn't politically correct, it's scientifically correct.

Because they provide a thin cloak of respectability for the racial prejudice that has yet to be rooted out of many parts of the United States and Europe, the theories of such as Herrnstein and Rushton continue to wield influence. Other genetic controversies, with a less explicit racial overtone but sometimes equally political, are conducted with as much ferocity. They centre on attempts to find genetic explanations for explicit human traits, rather than for broader patterns of low intelligence and under-achievement. Their implications are no less far-reaching, in that they too raise the question of what action should be taken as a result of the findings, should they turn out to be correct.

The knowledge that DNA (deoxyribonucleic acid) is the critical component of genes – a word that was itself only invented in 1909 – and Crick and Watson's identification of DNA's double-helix form in 1953, have been followed by the discovery of techniques of identification of specific genes which would allow intervention to abort a foetus if it was found to harbour undesirable characteristics, or even to alter those characteristics. Genetic engineering is already being used to improve animal and vegetable food crops. If it were ethically acceptable it could also be a means of breeding specific qualities into and out of the human race.

In February 1995 a closed conference was held at the Ciba Foundation in London to discuss whether criminal behaviour could be traced to genetic factors. It was inspired in part by the case of Stephen Mobley, sentenced to death in the American state of Georgia in 1991 for the murder of a pizza shop manager during a robbery. His lawyer sought a reprieve on the grounds that Mobley could not help being a killer, because there was a strong streak of violence in his genetic make-up. Mobley's aunt gave evidence that the Mobleys had been aggressive and violent for generations and that he came from a long line of convicted criminals – an argument that harked back to the nineteenth-century eugenicists who delighted in tracing patterns of criminal and other atypical behaviour back through extended families, preferably to one especially violent common ancestor. However, even this is not a conclusive argument for nature over nurture: it is surely impossible to determine whether somebody might be violent through heredity or because he or she had been subjected or exposed to violence as a child.

Mobley's lawyer, Daniel Summer, confessed that the idea for his novel defence plea came from reading about research carried out by Dutch scientists who, looking into the genetic make-up of a chronically criminal family, had discovered a mutation that caused an imbalance of chemicals in the brains of some male family members. Han Brunner, of the Department of Human Genetics at the University Hospital of Nijmegen, found that across four generations fourteen men in the family had been mentally retarded and unusually violent.

In this field, too, studies of twins have played an important role and several were referred to at the London conference. Professor Judy Silberg, of the Department of Human Genetics at Virginia Commonwealth University, studied 1,412 pairs of Caucasian twins aged eight to sixteen and found that some pairs displayed tendencies to misbehaviour and delinquency that she believes have genetic origins. Another study, by Dr Michael Lyons of Boston University, detected patterns of criminality in 3,200 pairs of male twins serving in the US armed forces. However, these studies suggested links only with non-violent criminal behaviour, and the conference agreed that it was harder to find a genetic 'cause' of violence.

The conference aroused strong opposition from many liberal scientists who oppose the theories of Shockley, Pearson, Rushton and Herrnstein. They believe the attempt to find genetic causes of social problems is an excuse for failing to tackle the environmental and educational failings that they believe to be the most important contributory factors. Patrick Bateson, Provost of King's College, Cambridge, gave the classic exposition of that position in an article in the London *Independent*:

> The development of individuals is an interplay between them and their environment. Individuals choose and change the conditions to which they are exposed; then they are themselves changed by those conditions. The prescription that all we have to do is locate the single, genetic cause of criminal behaviour and then get rid of it simply does not seem plausible.

That view was supported by Garland Allen, Professor of Biology at Washington University in St Louis, who told a meeting of the AAAS just after the Ciba conference:

> History shows that the genetic answer to sociological problems always has been used essentially against people. The genetic fix blames the biology of individuals rather than social circumstances for recurrent social and economic problems.

Steven Rose, Professor of Biology at Britain's Open University, attacked the conference because it gave what he saw as scientifically unacceptable research a veneer of respectability. Today it is recognised that there is a lot we do not understand about genetics and there is no guarantee at all that a child will replicate any of the qualities of its parents. Had the Nazis won the war and continued their eugenic experiment, the projected Master Race would still have been marred by a high proportion of deviant and imperfect specimens. (Dr Kleinle, who went into the Steinhöring home after the Americans liberated it, was struck by the number of children there who appeared backward in their development, but this may well have been the effect of long-term institutionalisation, as well as trauma caused by being moved from home to home as the war came to an end.)

The London conference was vigorously defended by its chairman, the child psychiatrist Sir Michael Rutter, in an interview with the London *Observer*. He said that nobody believed that genetic factors were the *only* causes of crime, but it was important to assess how strong the link was:

> It's biologically implausible to have a gene for something like crime, which is socially determined. It's like saying there's a gene for Roman Catholicism . . . We're dealing with a complex interaction of nature and nurture . . . The rise in crime and disorder over the last 50 years is clearly not genetic. Similarly, it's most unlikely that genetics plays a part in the fact that the murder rate among young people in the USA is more than 12 times that in this country. There are certain causal questions to which genetic research hasn't got anything useful to say.

Yet that emollient statement does not satisfy the critics of such research, who maintain that if you postulate even a partial genetic element in anti-social behaviour you raise questions about the use to which that theory is put. At a press conference before the London meeting, one of the participants, Dr Gregory Carey of the Institute of Behavioral Genetics at the University of Colorado, accepted the possibility that in time the presence of a 'criminal gene' might be detected by antenatal diagnosis, allowing the parents to choose to abort the child if they so wished.

Such an option edges dangerously close to the Nazi idea of 'racial health' and the elimination of people who might deviate from an arbitrary norm. As *The Times* of London had said in a leader eighteen months earlier:

If science can find a hereditary basis for traits such as criminality and violent aggression, political and ethical decisions will have to be made about how to deal with that knowledge.

That was in fact a comment on a different but related and even more sensitive issue. In 1993 Dr Dean Harries, a molecular geneticist at the US National Institute of Health, said his researches suggested the existence of a 'gay gene' present in many homosexuals. The findings received a mixed reception both from gays and others. On the one hand the research supported the contention of most gays that their sexuality is bred into them and is not a matter of perverse choice – just as Mobley's lawyer maintains that his client's criminality is bred into him. Yet it also meant that parents might one day be able to detect their child's future sexual proclivities before it is born and choose to abort the foetus if they are not satisfied with the findings. Should they be entitled to make that choice? How far can we go in manipulating the characteristics of the human race before we start believing that maybe Hitler's racial policies had some merit after all, and that the main fault may have been in their application and presentation?

Galton's original idea was seductively simple: that you could 'improve' humanity by breeding only from people whose qualities were by general consent thought to be worth preserving, and by discouraging or preventing reproduction among 'lesser' breeds – the very point of Shockley's sterilisation incentive scheme. In *Hereditary Genius* Galton wrote:

> Let us do what we can to encourage the multiplication of the races best fitted to invent and conform to a high and generous civilization and not, out of a mistaken instinct of giving support to the weak, prevent the incoming of strong and hearty individuals.

He appears not to have considered the possibility that his categorisation of people into 'the weak' and the 'strong and hearty' was not totally objective and that there would never be unanimity about what constitutes a greater or a lesser breed. This notion that his own subjective values – meaning those of the Victorian society he lived in – were unassailable was shared by the Nazis, who interpreted his exhortation 'let us do what we can' rather more broadly than he may have envisaged. Nobody can be expected to regard their own racial group, physical type or intellectual quality as so inferior that it should not be preserved. Therefore any attempt to give effect to a programme of eugenics will inevitably involve coercion and genocide.

The Nazis recognised this. Erich Koch, Reich-Commissioner for the Ukraine, said in Kiev in March 1943: 'No-one is willing to be stamped sub-human under the terror regime of a master race.' Yet they believed the ideal so worth attaining that they were prepared to pay the price of suppressing all their humanitarian instincts in its pursuit.

In *The Racial State*, Burleigh and Wippermann discuss whether the Nazis' racial policies were *sui generis*, or whether they were 'comparable with the crimes of other regimes, or indeed part of the "pathology" of advanced societies in general'. They take the former view, suggesting that those who hold to the latter 'would like us to believe that all our societies are latently like Nazi Germany'. They comment: 'Of course this is not so.' They describe Nazi Germany as 'a singular regime without precedent or parallel'.

But was it? People living through the horrors of modern war are inclined to comfort themselves with the thought that this time the lesson will be learned and that, as a result, nobody will again subject innocent people to such terrible excesses. Sadly, it never turns out like that. If the Nazi experience did not snuff out eugenics and 'scientific racism', still less did it put an end to racial conflict. Nearly all the wars that have scarred the globe in the second half of the twentieth century have been rooted in rivalry between peoples based on a conviction of racial superiority or victimisation. Although every member of the United Nations has signed the Genocide Convention, it is daily flouted in practice. In *The Roots of Evil*, Erwin Staub – a Jew who survived the Nazi occupation of Budapest – writes:

Genocides, mass killings and other cruelties inflicted on groups of people have not ceased since the Second World War. Consider the millions killed by their own people in Cambodia and Indonesia, the killing of the Hutu in Burundi, the Ibo in Nigeria, the Ache Indians in Paraguay, and the Buddhists in Tibet, and the mass killings in Uganda. Dictatorial governments have recently tended to kill not only individuals but whole groups of people seen as actual or potential enemies. This trend is evident in the Argentine disappearances and the death squad killings in El Salvador and Guatemala.

One significant point about Staub's list is that, with the exception of the South American examples, all the places he mentions were former colonies; except for Tibet, which is a colony still. While it would be an exaggeration to say that the natives were introduced to racial hatred by their colonial masters, they will certainly have observed how the representatives of the imperial power regarded themselves as innately superior by birth and breeding and protected themselves from social 'contamination' by strictly limiting their contacts with local people. They stuck chiefly to a master/servant relationship and regarded interracial sex and marriage with abhorrence. After independence this racial prejudice was reflected in the immigration policies of the former colonial powers and of most other developed countries.

It is surprising that Staub did not include South Africa on his list. After the National Party won the election there in 1948 it enacted a series of measures comparable to those passed by the Nazis in the thirties. In 1949 came an act prohibiting mixed marriages, in 1950 the Group Areas Act, underpinning apartheid, and in the same year legislation requiring people to register according to their race. Three years later the Reservation of Separate Amenities Act was passed, restricting non-whites to their own areas in public facilities such as parks, beaches and trains. In 1953 Dr Hendrik Verwoerd, the South African Prime Minister (and a Nazi supporter during the war), said:

There is no place for the Bantu in the European community above certain forms of labour ... For that reason it is of no avail for him to receive a training which has as its aim absorption into the European community.

Staub might also have included Switzerland where the racial theories and approach pioneered by Nazis such as Dr Ritter were employed to tackle its own gypsy 'problem'. Gypsy children were kidnapped from their parents and put into good Swiss homes to 'cleanse' them of their past. If the children resisted they were incarcerated and given electric shock treatment. If the parents tried to trace their children they were imprisoned or treated in mental homes. This programme, run by one of Switzerland's most famous children's charities, was operating as late as 1972.

Had Staub been writing in 1995 rather than in 1989, he would almost certainly have added to his list the former Yugoslavia, Czechoslovakia, Romania and Chechnya, and in Africa Rwanda as well as Burundi. At an International Congress of Genetics in Birmingham in August 1993, Sir Ralph Riley, former Secretary of the Agricultural and Food Research Council, touched on the ethnic conflict in the former nations of eastern Europe when he warned of the dangers of trying to improve the race through genetics:

> The racist Nazis, with their appalling genocide, and some of their contemporary successors, the ethnic cleansers, have chosen to believe that genetics is all-important in producing the ideal man and ideal society. This led in the past to some truly horrifying pseudo-genetical experimentation of which we must all feel ashamed. We must always be on our guard against the emergence of public policies with eugenic components.

It was not just the attempts to exterminate entire peoples that worried Sir Ralph, but what he called 'positive eugenics', which would involve fostering inherited qualities such as height and intelligence – and for that matter, although he did not mention it, heterosexuality. This would, he said, 'lead to infringement of human rights and would have unpredictable consequences for society'. There should be no public policy of promoting human characteristics regarded as desirable.

It was a timely warning that exposes the danger of too slavish an adherence to science and too great a reliance on the judgment of scientists. Scientific advances broaden the range of what is possible but not necessarily what is desirable. Even if we could effect profound and superficially beneficial changes to the human condition by genetic engineering, the Nazi experience teaches us that it should not be done except after the most responsible and broadly based consideration by others apart from scientists and those professionally involved in the field.

It is no use arguing that scientists today are so chastened that they would never go to the extremes described in this book. In *Exploding the Gene Myth*, Ruth Hubbard and Elijah Wald argue against the notion that German professionals under Hitler were somehow different from their counterparts in other times and places:

> Unfortunately, as many Germans remember, the Nazi programmes of eugenic 'selection and eradication' were designed and put in place by respected and respectable academics, jurists and heads of hospitals and scientific institutes. These people would be hard to distinguish from their present-day successors. They were just operating in a different political climate. In this country too, we must be vigilant and deliberate about what lines to draw and about who gets to draw them.

There will never be another Nazi Germany. Yet there will almost certainly be other attempts to use science to create illusory Utopias by the seductive notion of getting rid of 'them' and producing more people like us.

Select Bibliography

Ackermann, Josef: *Heinrich Himmler als Ideologe*, Müsterschmidt (Göttingen), 1970.

Baylis, William: *Caesars in Goosestep*, Harper, 1941.

Burleigh, M. and Wippermann, W: *The Racial State*, Cambridge University Press, 1991.

Coren, Michael: *The Invisible Man (The Life and Liberties of H. G. Wells)*, Bloomsbury, 1993.

Darwin Charles: *The Descent of Man*, London, 1871.

— *The Origin of Species*, John Murray, 1859.

Frischauer, Willi: *Himmler*, Odhams Press, 1953.

Galton, Francis: *Hereditary Genius*, London, 1869.

Gasman, Daniel: *The Scientific Origins of National Socialism*, New York, 1971.

Grunberger, Richard: *A Social History of the Third Reich*, Weidenfeld and Nicolson, 1971.

Haarer, Dr Johanna: *Die Deutsche Mutter und ihr erstes Kind*, Lehmann, Munich, 1940.

Hearnshaw, L. S: *Cyril Burt, Psychologist*, Cornell University Press, 1979.

Henry, Clarissa and Hillel, Marc: *Children of the SS*, Hutchinson, 1976.

Herrnstein, Richard: *I.Q. in the Meritocracy*, Allen Lane, 1973.

Herrnstein, Richard and Murray, Charles: *The Bell Curve*, Free Press, New York, 1994.

Hitler, Adolf: *Mein Kampf*, Munich, 1936.

Hrabar, Roman; Tokarz, Sofia; Wilczur, Jacek: *The Fate of Polish Children During the Last War*, Interpress (Warsaw), 1981.

Hubbard, Ruth and Wald, Elijah: *Exploding the Gene Myth*, Beacon Press, Boston, 1993.

Jones, Steve: *The Language of the Genes*, HarperCollins, 1993.

Kersten, Felix: *The Kersten Memoirs, 1940–5*, Hutchinson, 1956.

Keynes, Milo (ed.): *Sir Francis Galton FRS: The Legacy of His Ideas*, Macmillan, 1993.

Kühl, Stefan: *The Nazi Connection*, Oxford University Press, 1994.

Lilienthal, Georg: *Der Lebensborn, e.V.*, Fischer Verlag, Frankfurt, 1993.

Manvell, Roger and Fraenkel, Heinrich: *Heinrich Himmler*, Heinemann, 1965.

Mehr, Mariella: *Kinder der Landstrasse*, Zytglogg Berlag (Berne), 1987.

Neumann, Peter: *Other Men's Graves*, Weidenfeld & Nicolson, 1958.

Padfield, Peter: *Himmler*, Macmillan, 1990.

Poliakov, Leon: *The Aryan Myth, A History of Racist and Nationalist Ideas in Europe*, London, 1974.

Proctor, Robert: *Racial Hygiene: Medicine under the Nazis*, Harvard University Press, 1988.

Roberts, Stephen: *The House that Hitler Built*, Methuen, 1938.

Smith, Bradley and Peterson, Agnes (eds): *Heinrich Himmler Geheimreden*, Propylaen Verlag, 1974.

Staub, Erwin: *The Roots of Evil*, Cambridge University Press, 1989.

Time-Life Books: *The SS*, Time-Life, 1989.

Weindling, Paul: *Health, Race and German Politics Between National Unification and Nazism, 1870–1945*, Cambridge University Press, 1989.

Glossary

An explanation of the German words and initials that appear in the text:

Ahnenerbe: *Ancestral Heritage Society.*
BDM: *Bund deutscher Mädchen (League of German Girls).*
Freiherr: *Baron.*
Gauleiter: *Area commander.*
Gestapo: *Nazi secret police.*
Landtag: *Polish provincial assembly.*
Lebensborn: *Society for the care of selected mothers and babies of good racial stock (literally, fount of life).*
Lebensraum: *Literally, living space – the quest for it was used to justiify Germany's expansion eastwards.*
Lederhosen: *Traditional leather shorts worn in parts of Germany and Austria.*
Nazi: *National Socialist.*
NSDAP: *Nationalsozialistische deutsche Arbeiterpartei (full name of Nazi party).*
NSV: *Nationalsozialistische Volkswohlfahrt (National Socialist People's Welfare Organisation).*
Ostkinder: *Children from eastern European countries.*
Posen: *Poznan (Polish city).*
RKFDV: *Commission for Strengthening Germanism.*
Rassenhygiene: *Racial hygiene, or eugenics.*
Reich: *Empire.*
Reichsführer: *Imperial leader.*
Reichstag: *German Parliament from 1871 to 1945.*
RuSHA: *Race and Settlement Office.*
SA: *Sturmabteilung (Nazi storm troopers).*
SS: *Schutzstaffel: (élite Nazi security force).*
Stalag: *Prison camp.*
VOMI: *Office for the Repatriation of Ethnic Germans.*

Index

The glossary on page 199 explains German terms used in the book and in this index.

Index